The art of the ancient near east

e art of th

ncient near east

SETON LLOYD

THAMES AND HUDSON

Title page (1) Persepolis: detail of the procession of Medes and Persians from the audience-hall of Darius and Xerxes

Jacket, typographic design, and layout of the book by G. A. ADAMS

© THAMES AND HUDSON 1961

REPRINTED 1965

PRINTED IN GREAT BRITAIN BY JARROLD AND SONS LTD NORWIC

Contents

Introduction

In a world of equivocal values, art is an acceptable reality and its contemplation one of the greater privileges of our heredity. But its historical manifestations, numerous and varied as they are, have been 'sicklied o'er with the pale cast of thought'. Whole lifetimes have been spent in the study of some comparatively insignificant phase or 'movement'. In the present case, a moment's consideration of the subject which these pictures illustrate is sufficient to impress one with its magnitude and complexity. Like other studies of its sort, this is limited in time and place; but the two have here a special significance. The geographical area with which we are to deal provided a setting for man's earliest and greatest adventures in artistic expression; and our period of time witnessed prodigies of intellectual development without parallel in his subsequent history.

For it was not only art which had its beginnings in the Near East during the remote age we are about to describe. Science followed hard on the invention of writing: superstition was replaced by ordered religion and philosophy. In the space of no more than a few centuries humanity acquired the power of self-expression, and learnt to enrich the world with the products of its own ingenuity. It is an extraordinary story of spontaneous creation, and all the more remarkable for the comparatively short time in which the whole transformation took place. Two thousand years before Greek civilization was heard of, Near Eastern man had already become familiar with the subtleties of intellectual understanding. When Sophocles spoke of our most advanced achievements—'language and wind-swift thought and city-dwelling habits'—he was referring to a heritage of whose antiquity he had no conception. Nor, for that matter, had we ourselves until comparatively recent years. For it is by no means generally realized how much the historian's view of such matters has changed in our own lifetime.

7

Half a century ago the very history of the ancient Near East was imperfectly known. Much of the evidence which today makes its understanding possible had not yet been discovered; and in the realm of art it should be remembered that this includes rather more than half of the objects illustrated in this book. It is also interesting to recall the popular attitude at the end of the last century to such works as were already known or had recently been discovered. The Egyptian monuments, the Assyrian reliefs, and other antiquities of a character too insistently obtrusive to be ignored were regarded with curiosity rather than admiration. They were thought of, like the newly deciphered inscriptions which accompanied them, as being vaguely associated with Biblical history and invested generally with the glamour of extreme antiquity. But to minds conditioned by nineteenth-century education, the forms of artistic expression and intellectual ideas which they represented, seemed archaic, alien, and even grotesque; a kind of 'false start' or premature and abortive development in art, unconnected in any way with the true genesis of our own culture which was associated with classical Greece.

Today all this is changed completely, and our reference to Greece has a special relevance in considering the main factors which have changed it. Our own thinking is connected with that of the ancient Greeks by such an unbroken thread of tradition that almost every aspect of their civilization can perfectly be understood. In the case of the ancient Near East the very reverse is true. A considerable literature has already accumulated on the subject of its various civilizations, but it is based almost exclusively on the study of their material remains which have been discovered by archaeologists during the past century.

It depends, that is, primarily on archaeology. For if this word be used in its more comprehensive sense, it must be taken to include the manifold activities of a versatile and diversely occupied profession, the dual function of which is first to make available historical evidence and secondly to be concerned with its interpretation. Indeed, in the Near East archaeology has provided a kind of 'lens', through which today these ancient civilizations have become more clearly visible against their correct geographical and historical background, and their monuments are now recognizable as works of art. In these circumstances the present writer has little need to apologize for being in fact a professional archaeologist.

Having said this much, an important reservation must be made in regard to the quality and completeness of our newly acquired knowledge. The pictures presented in this book are no more than a small representative collection of art-works, chosen for their conspicuous beauty or having some other special significance. The present assemblage could easily be duplicated or its contents multiplied many times over without beginning to exhaust the available choice or supply. Yet the total of existing antiquities from which these are selected is no more than a chance residue—microscopically small— of the vast wealth accumulated in their time by the ancient peoples we are considering. From this same modest total of remains, supplemented by equally small relics of their literature, the daily lives, mental processes, and general behaviour, as well as the actual history of those peoples have been reconstructed with astonishing ingenuity and perception by modern scholars. Yet their conclusions may no more be considered complete or even adequate than the volume of evidence on which they are based. In a word, then, there is still a great deal about these ancient peoples that we do not know. There are also many of their surviving works which we simply do not understand, though the fault in this case often lies in the circumstances of their discovery.

In archaeology, the scholar is dependent for his interpretation on the excavator's account of the setting in which an object was found; but both are frustrated by commercial traffic in antiquities which destroys their value as documents. Perhaps all this will serve to explain why references to archaeological matters must occur so frequently in a work which should otherwise be directly concerned with art-history. Certainly, if we return now as we must to the birth of civilization in the Near East and to the first beginnings of art, our inquiry will have to be directed through archaeological channels.

Prehistorians in our own generation have familiarized us with the successive phases through which the civilizing process passed: the transition from a food-gathering to a food-producing economy;

the first sporadic attempts at systematic farming and the 'Neolithic revolution' which substituted the ordered life of settled communities for the precarious improvisations of nomadic existence. Among the people of that age it brought into being new social classes, such as the artisans whose special contribution excused them from agricultural labour, or the story-tellers and musicians with their gift for stimulating man's thoughts about himself. Next came the federation of village entities for mutual help or protection and the recognition of one of them as leader. The idea of a city, with its prospect of even greater complexity and the political organization of a city-state were by then not far distant.

The final and decisive steps in man's progress from Neolithic adolescence to the full maturity of civilized emancipation seems to have depended not only on the initiative of precocious minorities but also, and to an even greater extent, on the effect produced by particular forms of environment. Indeed, the genesis of the whole extraordinary phenomenon would be a great deal more easily explained if it could be conveniently attributed to the inborn genius of some well-defined racial group—to a 'chosen people' in the Old Testament sense. But this clearly is not the case; since the Sumerians for instance of Lower Mesopotamia and the early dynasts of the Nile Valley, who shared the honours with them in this respect, were racially and otherwise quite unrelated. It is rather then in the countries themselves that we must seek some common factor which may have stimulated their rapid development.

During the fifth and fourth millennia B.C., a slow prelude to fulfilment was played out in the Near East by prehistoric peoples of mixed extraction, who appear to have been fairly widely distributed. Certainly the lands in which they dwelt included Egypt, Palestine, Syria, and Mesopotamia; a girdle of cultivable lands encircling the wilderness of Arabia once designated by James Henry Breasted the 'fertile crescent'.

In our picture of the early world, this shapeless terrain with its varied climate appears for a score of centuries to accommodate a congregation of peoples, whose united ambition is limited to the maintenance of a simple agricultural economy in villages loosely grouped on tribal principles. This age of innocence prolongs itself almost until the end of the fourth millennium, but ends in an astonishing transformation. In a space of time which can almost be reckoned in generations, the entire scene changes. Cities are founded and new systems of government contrived for them; religious beliefs and observances are formulated. The art of writing appears as a novel invention, accompanied by monumental architecture, sculpture, and the first experiments in science. It is as though the whole potential of human ingenuity had quite suddenly been fully understood and unhesitatingly exploited.

If this is to be taken as the point in man's history at which civilization in the accepted sense begins, let us consider once more the geographical location of its birth. From its inception the whole remarkable development is strictly localized. As Oswald Spengler observed—'It comes into flower on the soil of precisely definable regions, to which it remains linked by a plant-like attachment.' Furthermore, and even more strangely, an almost identical blossoming appears to have taken place simultaneously in two widely separated localities. The glow of partial enlightenment, which has hitherto been fairly evenly diffused over the countries of the Near East, seems suddenly concentrated in the brilliant illumination of two individual provinces: Egypt and Mesopotamia.

We shall deal then with these two great centres of world civilization jointly at first, since their early developments were along such closely parallel lines. Next we shall discuss separately their progress during the formative period in the first half of the third millennium B.C. in which their cultural growth reached maturity, and notice the regional characteristics by which it was now so sharply differentiated. Other countries of the Near East will after that have to be considered. Persia will have already been mentioned in connexion with the heredity of the Sumerians. Anatolia and countries of the Levant, Syria, and Palestine will appear as the home of peripheral cultures, whose contribution to the total of creative accomplishment in the Near East was of minor importance and their art a dim light reflected from more brilliant constellations.

And in all this, because our deliberations will depend on the understanding of man as a reflective being, we shall find his desire for artistic expression intimately associated with his religious beliefs. For in the whole of the ancient Near East, art was inseparable from religion and without it would have found little inspiration. Indeed, the works of a purely profane character illustrated in this book form such a negligible minority, that a word should at once be said about the principles of Near Eastern theology which make the rest to a greater or lesser degree comprehensible.

One cardinal preoccupation of primitive religious thought, common to both Egypt and Mesopotamia, consists in speculation regarding the purpose of human life and the creation of the world into which man is born. In both countries the first and simplest concept is that of initial 'chaos', out of which 'order' is brought and a coherent pattern of life established through the grace of a dimly conceived original spirit. Both peoples also pictured the universe as a formless and limitless expanse of darkness, referred to by the Egyptian word meaning 'waters' and the primeval 'abyss' of Mesopotamian imagery. Both also agree on the emergence from the waters of a primordial 'mound' or platform, an idea which was for them perhaps associated with islands of mud left by the receding Nile floods or the reclamation of land from the tidal marshes of Sumer. But the Egyptians also conceived an alternative picture of a three-dimensional 'abyss', in which a light and habitable area opened like an envelope or bubble, limited on all sides by the primeval 'waters'. And this introduces us for the first time to the strangely undisciplined fluidity of Egyptian thinking, where conflicting notions could exist side-by-side without sense of contradiction, like multiple hypotheses in a single complex speculation.

From an early stage, separate forces in the performance of this miracle were recognizable by names or symbols. The primary creator-spirit became the first of the 'Great Gods', Atum-Ra. Conceived of as hermaphrodite, he procured for himself a supplementary pair of spirits, and they in their turn begat the twin elements of earth and sky, which when separated shaped the 'firmament'. Shu and Tefnut—Geb and Nut—their names are perhaps unimportant to the lay reader, except inasmuch as their relationship shaped itself into an immutable formula which survived as the basis of Egyptian belief and ritual for several thousand years. However it may have been modified and complicated by later accretions, the central liturgy continued to be compounded of the same unchanging elements, and it was to these that the planning of temples was invariably accommodated. Rundle Clark has in this respect compared them to the Christian Church which, through all the vicissitudes of factional deviation, has retained its primary function as a setting for the Holy Eucharist.

In Egyptian beliefs there are two other determinative principles, one of which is the concept of divine kingship. This also seems to have been foreshadowed by the creation-formula, in which the primeval 'mound' is sometimes alternatively described as a 'throne'. Certainly the assurance and control of man's fortunes by a beneficent god, through the intervention of an earthly ruler who was in fact his own provisional incarnation, was accepted from the earliest historic times onwards as part of the 'order' which creation brought out of 'chaos'. The Egyptian Pharaoh was thus invested with all the attributes most satisfying to his subjects—National Hero—Leading Warrior—figurative 'Son of the Gods'; in fact the manifestation on earth of God himself.

Secondly the Egyptians seem to have been obsessed with the possibilities of immortality and life-after-death. This was at first perhaps dependent on their identification of kingship with divinity for it manifests itself in the elaborate provision of funerary equipment for royal tombs. But similar privileges are later extended to the Pharaoh's less exalted subjects, the prolongation of whose life after death in a modified form was also provided for. There is an almost macabre materialism in the form which these provisions took; in the supply of comforts and amenities, undifferentiated in any way from the requirements of a mere mortal. And it is therefore hardly surprising that, as metaphysical speculation increased, some more abstract objective for human aspirations came to be sought. In the course of time this need was met by the cult of the god Osiris.

By the end of the Egyptian Fifth Dynasty, in about 2500 B.C., we have a new form of evidence for Egyptian religious beliefs in the form of the so-called Pyramid Texts—the earliest preserved body of religious literature, which is largely a product of the famous Heliopolitan school of theology. The cult of Osiris here emerges as a newly instituted form of what may broadly be called nature-worship, and from now onwards it continues to exist concurrently with other and sometimes rival cults. It is at first a 'fertility cult', similar to those found in all parts of the Near East from the earliest times, in which the male Osiris is associated with a consort, Isis and a son, Horus in a triple formula with an obvious significance. But as a 'dying god', Osiris came later to be connected with the after-life, and so by gradual degrees with a spiritual destiny distinct from mere material persistence.

But in deference to the Egyptian tradition of theological complexity, older beliefs and practices were by no means superseded, and the cult of Osiris came to be considered merely as a single facet in the structure of a composite faith. The Great Gods continued to be pre-eminent in their own spheres, which varied in importance only with the shift of political ascendancy from one religious centre to another. In Heliopolis the sun-god, Ra, was still the supreme deity at the end of the Old Kingdom: Amen of Thebes usurped his position in the Middle Kingdom and maintained it (with a short interval for heretical Aten-worship) until the end of the New. But these were merely the central figures in an ever-increasing tangle of sub-deities, nature-spirits, and other mythological creations, which was further complicated by the tendency for each to have several different manifestations, or for two to become assimilated without losing their identity.

Such then were the primary characteristics which distinguished Egyptian religion from that of Mesopotamia and other neighbouring countries. For the Sumerian king was a mere 'leader' or 'shepherd' of his people, and in relation to his god no more than a 'steward'. Nor was the Sumerian, or for that matter any other contemporary religion much concerned with life-after-death. Outside Egypt there is a lack of funerary evidence to confirm this generalization, but in Mesopotamian religious literature and art, this subject seems to be so overshadowed by the hazards of human existence that there is time

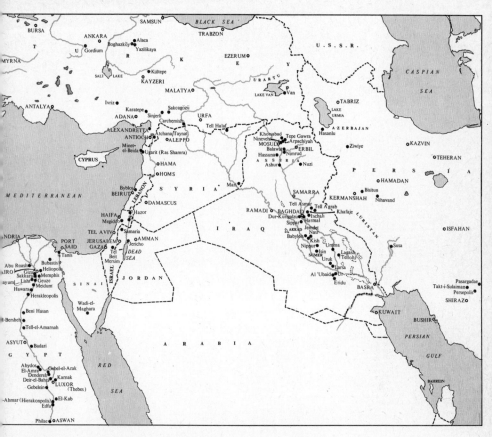

2 Map showing the main areas and sites important for the history of art in the ancient Near East: modern towns are capitalized, sites are shown in upper and lower case

for no more than a resentful glance at the threat of mortality. Certainly the realm of spiritual survival, dimly located 'among the stars' in the Osiride conception, sounds superior to the dark and formless purgatory of the Sumerian 'underworld'. But here again is an outstandingly important subject, still insufficiently documented or understood for us to be able to do more than speculate about it. We must content ourselves with pictorial scenes, such as that of a Sumerian ruler modestly confronting his god or a Hittite king in the protective embrace of a young deity, and with our own ability to savour in them the religious climate of so remote an age.

But our text and the pictures which illustrate it will make these things clear. Here it remains only for the writer to discharge a personal obligation.

Belonging as I do to the class of archaeologist whose duties have lain mainly in the field of excavation, I have sought help in my argument from those pre-eminent in the realm of interpretation. Above all my debt is to Henri and H. A. G. Frankfort, whose scholarly and imaginative writing I have frequently quoted, because their well-tempered idiom can seldom be paraphrased. To these two names should be added that of Cyril Aldred, since his skilful and elegantly worded summary in *Ancient Egyptian Art* has been drawn upon to fill the gaps in my own knowledge. Finally I am also indebted to my wife for advice on aesthetics, and to Mr Harry Smith of Christ's College, Cambridge, for help of the sort which only an Egyptologist could give.

PART ONE

Egypt and Sumer:
The Stimulus of Environment

This story of a momentous sequel to the genesis of mankind may be thought of as resembling a Nativity play. When the spectacle is introduced, the curtain first rises to reveal a picture of the Near East, in which two countries only are as yet illuminated. Egypt and Mesopotamia emerge separately from the surrounding obscurity, their familiar anatomy already easily recognizable.

The geological formation of these two great river-valleys, and the history of their early population by human beings have much in common but also some notable differences. To understand the beginnings of life in Egypt one has to picture, during the Neolithic period, the gradual drying-up of North Africa and the Levant, until the great elongated canyon through which the Nile flowed and the delta which it was gradually creating, alone remained like an oasis of inhabitable humidity. Upon this haven converged not only tribes of Neolithic farmers, but a countless variety of wild animals and birds. The first cultivators settled in the meadows and shrublands which emerged from the mud-flats as the river continually altered its course. Their isolated villages were surrounded by marshlands of rushes or sedge and forests of tall papyrus. Here and in the parkland of the tributary *wadis* on either side of the valley, the villagers found themselves in intimate relationship with the teeming wild-life, which shared their new home. Meat was plentiful for habitual hunters, and a surprising variety of species seems to have been deemed suitable for domestication. The effects of this early intimacy with the fauna so confidently sharing their environment are still to be seen in the zoological symbolism of Egyptian religion in historical times and its sensitive iconography.

Archaeological remains of these earliest settlers have been found, not in the valley itself, where the flood-water has long ago removed

3 These vessels from Susa and Persepolis are decorated in lustrous black paint, fading to wine-colour, on a wet-smoothed yellowish ground. Prehistoric animal and bird drawings have been through a long process of formalization, culminating in these well-adapted decorative motifs for panel-filling or surface ornament

or buried them beneath its falling burden of alluvial mud, but in recesses of the escarpments which enclosed the valley on either side. They have once more provided details of the prelude to Egyptian history in the fifth and early fourth millennia B.C., which Egyptologists divide into three phases, conveniently named after the sites where traces of them were found; Tasian, Badarian, and Amratian. Between the last of these and the actual foundation of the first Pharaonic dynasty in about 3100 B.C., there is a final Predynastic phase called Gerzean. This Gerzean period is of immensely greater significance, since it witnessed the first vital stages in the upsurge of cultural creativity which is our subject. The material evidence in this respect is unhappily meagre, yet it suffices to show that most elements which eventually contributed to the maturity of Dynastic civilization were already present at this period.

In Mesopotamia a phase of comparable significance is immediately apparent in the so-called Protoliterate period; an epoch rather

awkwardly labelled in this way because the art of writing is already known, though hardly as yet used for monumental purposes. Covering the six or seven centuries which precede the beginnings of written history, it not only fits chronologically with the Gerzean period in Egypt, but is distinguished by the same convulsive cultural developments, with which are associated the first considerable manifestations of creative art. These make their appearance almost simultaneously in the two milieux; but in such clear independence and isolation that in comparing them presently we shall be struck more than anything by the factors in their character which are inexplicably but unmistakably common to both.

In Mesopotamia, the whole cultural development of which we are speaking is usually attributed to the precocious ability of the Sumerians—a non-Indo-European, non-Semitic people whose presence in the alluvial province created by the Lower Tigris and Euphrates is attested historically from the beginning of the third

19

millennium onwards. Today very little doubt any longer exists regarding their origins. They were the first arrivals in the drying marshes at the head of the Persian Gulf, and they came down from an earlier home in the Iranian Highlands, where their remoter past merges into a pattern of prehistoric migrations. Their new homeland resembled in many respects that of the first Egyptians in the Nile Valley. Their settlements were raised on islands or banks of mud emerging from reedy marshes; for agriculture they depended both on the annual flooding of the rivers and on irrigation; like the Marsh-Arabs of modern Iraq they domesticated cattle of the water-buffalo type and they hunted lions, boar, or wildfowl and fished like the Egyptians. Clay and reeds were the most handy material for all purposes; and if their talent for painting pottery was perhaps no more remarkable than the attainments of earlier craftsmen elsewhere, their astonishingly rapid mastery of architectural design and ornament, first through the elaboration of reed-and-clay structures and later of bricks and terracotta, is just one of those symptoms of inborn originality which was to raise them head and shoulders above their primitive contemporaries.

But here we are reaching too far ahead. We must start at the beginning by seeking out and considering the very earliest germination in Near Eastern man of a capacity for spontaneous artistic expression. This will mean returning for a moment to the semi-static world of the prehistoric peoples; and we shall there immediately find ourselves handicapped by the comparative scarcity of material evidence. At first glance indeed, there appear to be no more than two categories of artifact worth considering. One is pottery and the other prehistoric figurines of men or animals. The former, being ubiquitous and almost indestructible, offers the more considerable volume of evidence and is most rewarding as a subject of study.

It is generally assumed that the design of baked clay vessels provided a first outlet for the impulse in man to create something with an aesthetically satisfying appearance. Craftsmen of a very early age must have observed that the utility of their products need not be impaired by minor adjustments of shape for this purpose. Such experiments would lead naturally to the addition of surface ornament;

and incised patterns reminiscent of the vessel's basketwork origin might suggest an easy beginning. It could at first be no more than a fanciful gesture which brought a band of bright paint to the rim of a bowl; but when falling drops traced vertical lines from rim to base, new decorative possibilities would become apparent. Tentative patterns began to emerge, simple at first and as a rule rigidly geometrical, but later developing freedom and subtlety which permitted of their adaptation to plastic form.

Yet it would almost certainly be wrong to conclude that these earliest experiments in two-dimensional ornament were confined exclusively to pottery. As the designs evolve and their motifs multiply, intrusive elements, peculiar for instance to the process of weaving cloth, are occasionally recognizable and can be seen to impose a character alien to the principles of painted ornament. The consequent conclusion that already at this early period simple products of the loom were commonly supplemented by pattern-stitching, has recently come to be widely accepted, and is indeed substantiated by actual finds such as a woven skirt knotted with beads, from an Al 'Ubaid grave at Eridu (c. 3500 B.C.). From prehistoric excavations in the Near East there is a vast and varied assemblage of material to illustrate such developments, and examples can be chosen almost at random. As for the supposed influence of textiles, it can perhaps most clearly be seen in the early 'Eridu' pottery of southern Mesopotamia and in the polychrome Tell Halaf ware of the north (Ill. 5). Certainly in Persia, by the time the historic period is reached, painted ornament on pottery is often almost indistinguishable from traditional designs used in weaving kileems and other modern fabrics (Ill. 4).

It is from Persia that archaeologists derive the finest ceramic ornament associated with this period: and there can be no doubt that the kind of designs which develop spontaneously from the use of paint on a soft brush are best illustrated by examples of prehistoric pottery from sites like Susa and Persepolis (Ill. 3). Their bold curves and contrasting angularities are beautifully adapted to plastic requirements and improved by wide spacing. Furthermore they provide a feature of peculiar interest in the adoption of bird, animal,

4 Nihavand: painted jar of mid second millennium B.C. showing the use in Persia during the historic period of designs, including animal motifs properly belonging to textiles. In this example they make a striking comparison with comparatively modern *kileem* or rug patterns

and even human forms as decorative motifs. There is here perhaps a distant connexion with the cave-paintings of Palaeolithic man: but if so, a link is still missing and must be sought in unknown intermediate developments. For when we reach the earliest Susa designs, the shapes are already stylized almost beyond recognition. The simplified silhouettes of animals and birds, like the dancing homunculi which must once have featured as individual figures, are even linked together in a repetitive frieze, to form a band of enrichment or to emphasize the horizontal significance of some plastic curve. Here and there one still sees an isolated figure, whose sole function is to fill a gap in the design: like the hunter with his bow in *Ill. 6*

5 Tell Halaf ware; the pottery is burnished after firing to give it a slight polish. The designs used show the influence of basketwork or perhaps once again of textile patterns

who might equally well have been found on the wall of a cave. But by contrast, the ibex-symbol in this picture is recognizable merely as a decorative unit, purposely adapted to the panel in which it is set. Like other representations of animals and birds, its very identity has become irrelevant, since the painter himself, concerned only with its decorative value, may well have been ignorant of its traditional significance.

These early vase-painters mark a stage at which regional characteristics in the development of art begin to be differentiated. Where Persia is concerned, we shall presently examine some of the qualities by which local art-forms are distinguished in later times. They

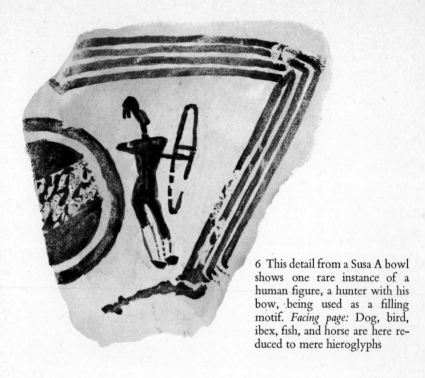

6 This detail from a Susa A bowl shows one rare instance of a human figure, a hunter with his bow, being used as a filling motif. *Facing page:* Dog, bird, ibex, fish, and horse are here reduced to mere hieroglyphs

include for instance a peculiar clarity and precision in the ordered arrangement of decorative shapes; a predilection for expressive silhouettes and a conspicuous interest in birds and animals (*Ill. 6*). Comparable traits, as we have seen, can already clearly be detected in the ceramic ornament of the prehistoric period in Persia; and we shall accordingly be led to conclude that these are deep-seated regional idiosyncrasies, contributing to a tradition in art which is to all intents and purposes indestructible. It seems probable that, if more was known of the early history of music, traces of the same conservatism could be found there also.

If something is to be learnt from regional development in pottery, the same cannot unfortunately be said of prehistoric figurines. The form they take and their diverse peculiarities indicate as a rule the period to which they belong rather than the place they come from. Of the animal figures the great majority are crudely made playthings for children and of no artistic interest. Those on the other hand which are based upon the human form or provided with recognizably human attributes, have a magic or religious significance that places them in the category of cult-objects (*Ill. 7*). Their main distinction lies in the fact that they seek to give plastic expression to an abstract idea or symbol. But the shapes which confront us have become so stereotyped that their meaning is almost completely lost to us (as it may ultimately well have been to those who made them). Indeed so remote from modern understanding has their archaic symbolism become, that anthropologists content themselves with generalizations about the personification of fertility and the Asiatic 'mother-goddess'. Nor in these circumstances is much to be gained

from any attempted interpretation of their plastic detail: the imagery of so remote an age is too obscure (*Ill. 7–10*).

The objects to which we have been referring belong in Mesopotamia to the Al 'Ubaid phase. The later half of this phase is also distinguished by the earliest experiments in formal architecture; and these seem to testify to an interest in design which could no longer be satisfied by ornamental pottery. Some indeed would see in them evidence that the Sumerians have already appeared on the scene; but whether or not this is so, as the generations pass, which separate the vase-painters of Al 'Ubaid from the great innovators of Protoliterate Mesopotamia and Predynastic Egypt, the cultural upheaval can be seen to be gaining momentum.

First we must refer to the invention during this period of the art of writing, which again seems to have developed independently in

7 Naqada: two Egyptian Predynastic figurines of the Gerzean culture, the left of ivory, the right of alabaster. These are still no more than primitive totems

the two countries. There is evidence to suggest that its first appearance in Mesopotamia should be dated a shade earlier than in Egypt, and—what is perhaps more interesting—that the purposes for which it was first used were by no means identical. In Mesopotamia the earliest writing took the form of administrative records and served a strictly practical purpose; in Egypt it appears in the shape of commemorative texts on royal monuments. The beginning of Egyptian history therefore coincides exactly with the invention of writing;

 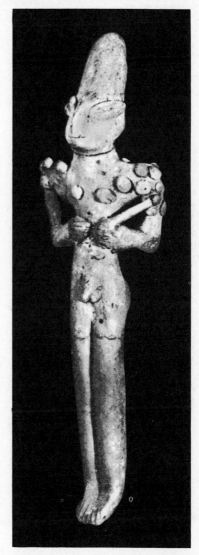

8 *Left:* Terracotta figurine from the Predynastic levels at Al 'Ubaid with a bitumen wig and incised pubic triangle. Excrescences on the shoulders may represent tattooing.   9 *Right:* A male figurine of the same type from Eridu, carrying an emblematic mace

and we are consequently able to gather something about political events in Predynastic times. We see the Egyptians of that period as a homogeneous people, loosely grouped in rural districts dependent on small market-towns, and already intelligently exploiting their rich agricultural environment. Politically, however, a distinction is made between 'Upper' and 'Lower' Egypt, which have their own separate kings. They are military rivals, perpetually covetous of each other's territory. The names of some of them appear in reliefs, but have to be identified by the hieroglyphic forms which they take (such as 'Scorpion' or 'Snake'), since we do not know how they were pronounced. For the rest it is possible to conclude that the people of Upper Egypt had predominantly African characteristics, derived no doubt from their forebears and contemporary associations; whereas Lower Egypt tended to be influenced by the ideas and material assets of their Asiatic neighbours.

Where Predynastic art is concerned, there are again already regional distinctions. Egyptian artists are mainly concerned with historical and monumental subjects, while Protoliterate art in Mesopotamia is primarily religious. In Egypt the actual monuments surviving from the period are by no means plentiful, but they make up for this by their truly remarkable character. Their monumental intent is in almost all cases obvious, since the descriptive scenes depicted are in fact 'reminders' of historical events, and as such the precursors of written history. They consist mostly of fine carvings in relief on stone or ivory. A huge votive mace-head in the Ashmolean Museum (*Ill. 11*) commemorates the conquests of an Upper Egyptian king, 'Scorpion', who is for some reason depicted supervising the opening of a canal. This king seems to have succeeded in consolidating the Upper Egyptian Kingdoms as far north as Cairo; for his monuments have been found near there in the Turah quarries. Then there are the beautiful ivory knife-handle from Gebel-el-Arak in Upper Egypt (*Ill. 12*), depicting the pursuit of game, and a number of sculptured stone palettes—objects which must originally have had a practical purpose in holding eye-pigment, but which have somehow acquired a monumental function. There are also the 'Hunter's palette' in the British Museum (*Ill. 13*),

28

10 Naqada: dancing figurine of the Egyptian Predynastic Amratian culture. The slender form unlike the stylized Gerzean figures recognizes the significance of human anatomy. The rough painted designs are a combination of geometric patterns, representations of dress ornament—or perhaps tattooing—and semi-naturalistic animal forms

11 Hierakonopolis: two ceremonial votive limestone mace-heads. The larger mace shows King 'Scorpion' ceremonially opening a canal. He wears the white crown of Upper Egypt and a kilt with an animal tail and is accompanied by a retinue. The figures are not yet placed on groundlines and the curve of the irrigation canal and awkward position of the kneeling figure with the basket are clumsy attempts to represent three-dimensional space

12 Gebel-el-Arak: obverse and reverse of an ivory-handled flint knife, illustrating the earliest Egyptian relief-carving. The figure supported by two lions in the hunting scene makes a striking comparison with the Mesopotamian archer in *Ill. 17*, while the naked figures in the battle scene are almost identical with those on the Sumerian stone vase (*Ill. 18*)

13 The Predynastic 'Hunter's palette' in slate with a central mixing panel shows two groups co-operating in a lion-hunt; they wear head-feathers and kilts and carry various weapons. On the lower right-hand fragment one of their number has a lasso. Compare with *Ill. 17*

on which two groups of people, distinguished by standards, collaborate in what must have been a traditionally famous lion-hunt; and others with wild animals and more fantastic beasts, whose significance for the most part escapes us. Finally, though it does not properly belong to the period, there is the famous 'Narmer palette' (*Ill. 14*)—a twofold monument, commemorating a royal victory and the final amalgamation of Upper and Lower Egypt under a single ruler. For the ancient Egyptians traced their history back to Menes, the first king of their First Dynasty, who ruled at Nekhen (Hierakonopolis), and who traditionally united the whole land into a single Kingdom. Narmer and Menes are now generally considered to be identical.

Taken in sequence, these sculptured reliefs represent the earliest stages of Egyptian art. The knife-handle, for instance, shows a pattern of figures which, in their arbitrary horizontal arrangement, have hardly even begun to conform to the outline of the object

14 Hierakonopolis: the votive palette of King Narmer, perhaps the first sovereign to unite the 'Two Lands' under a single rule, is a key monument of the Archaic period. *Right:* The King wearing the crown of Lower Egypt and preceded by his standards, goes out to inspect the enemy dead. Entwined beasts below appear also in Sumerian art. At the bottom the King in the form of a wild ox batters down the door of a fortified settlement. *Left:* On the reverse the King, now wearing the southern crown, strikes down a kneeling enemy. At the bottom are two fallen enemies

which they decorate. Yet they are no longer isolated or aimlessly scattered in the manner of cave-paintings. They are purposefully grouped and related to make a coherent scene. All these carvings show outstanding craftsmanship, fine drawing of organic shapes and—what is more important—an understanding of their adaptability to the requirements of abstract design. In this respect they are entirely without parallel in any form of prehistoric art. But their secondary

33

15 Hierakonopolis: wall-painting from a tomb showing an expansion of the themes shown on the Gebel-el-Arak knife even to a naval scene which appears on the reverse of the knife-handle. The African animals and their mythical counterparts are woven into a pattern with no apparent monumental purpose

interest lies in the fact that the principles to which they conform still have little in common with those of Egyptian art in later times. They have the function of 'illustrations', in contrast to the formal 'statements' of classical practice. In the mace-head, for example, the shape of the canal features as a clumsy device, aimed at creating a space-relationship between the figure of the King and those of his assisting subordinates. By the time we reach the Narmer palette, the need for such an expedient has already been avoided by the device known as a 'groundline', which divides the picture into simple horizontal registers—a formula afterwards rigidly adhered to for many centuries. Unlike King 'Scorpion', whose bodily appearance on a specific occasion is depicted on the mace-head, King Narmer's gesture of slaying an enemy acquires the static quality of a symbol, endlessly repeated in the subsequent history of Egyptian art.

Two more Predynastic monuments, representing media other than carving, must be mentioned. One is the astonishing wall-painting from Kom-el-Ahmar, the site of Hierakonopolis (*Ill. 15*);

34

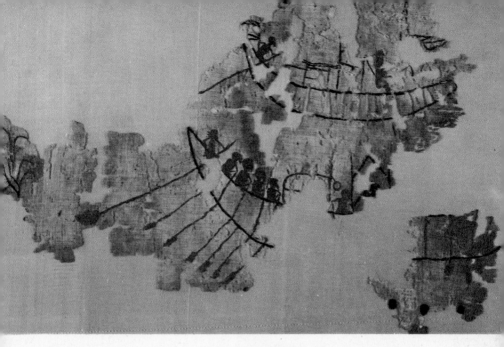

16 El-Gebelein: fragments of painted linen from a Predynastic tomb showing a hippopotamus-hunt taking place from two different-sized vessels. Unlike most representations of human figures at the time these have short noses and wear beards

the other is the fragmentary painted fabric from Gebelein (*Ill. 16*)—surely the most ancient relic of its sort that has survived. The wall-painting seems to be half-way in conception between the Predynastic carvings and the Narmer palette. In it all the main stylistic developments of the period seem to be represented in miniature. As in the Gebel-el-Arak carving, individual figures in the foreground are grouped and connected, by 'intent' (sparring warriors), 'action' (slaying an enemy—or *enemies*, when the plural is expressed graphically), or by 'interest' (a stag looking back over its shoulder). The heraldic device of a human figure supported by pairs of beasts again echoes the dominant group on the knife-handle. The five animals in the centre (said to be 'caught in a trap') make a centrifugal pattern more reminiscent of prehistoric pottery, but those above are already unmistakably linked by a groundline as in the Narmer palette. Works of this sort from Hierakonopolis, character-istic of the first formative stages of Egyptian art, are so instructive and significant that one hopes the excavations may eventually be

17 Warka (Uruk). Granite stela and detail (*right*) of Protoliterate period depicting a lion-hunt. The comparison with contemporary Egyptian carving is significant. The two huntsmen bearded, long-haired, wearing a head-band and broad belted kilt recall the heraldic group on the Gebel-el-Arak knife-handle (*Ill. 12*), the impaled lions those on the 'Hunter's palette' (*Ill. 13*)

continued. The Gebelein textile too shows an early Egyptian aptitude for visual expression, for which little scope is afforded by the conventions of later times.

Art-objects which have survived from earliest Sumerian times in Mesopotamia are hardly more plentiful than the relics of Predynastic Egypt. They consist exclusively of stone-carvings, either in relief or in the round; and, considering the extreme rarity of stone in the alluvial plain of southern Iraq, we should be grateful for the widespread archaeological enterprise to which we owe their recovery. Two of the best-known and earliest examples are from Warka (ancient Uruk). These at once illustrate the adaptability of the sculptor's technique to varying materials, the one being of granite and the other alabaster. The first is a fragmentary stela, on which a hunting scene is depicted (*Ill. 17*); the second a tall stone vase, carved in horizontal registers with an elaborate religious scene

(*Ill. 18*). If, after so sudden a transition from one geographical milieu to another, we compare these carvings with their Egyptian counterparts, we are struck by a similarity so remarkable that we find it hard to believe in their independent origin. In the first place, the depth and quality of the relief-carving is indistinguishable, and only in the case of the granite fragment is its precision slightly dulled by the technical limitations of the material. Next, there are the subjects chosen and the actual figures composing them. That of the 'Lion-hunt' recalls the Hunter's palette; and no one can fail to observe that, apart from any more general similarity in the scene depicted, the lions themselves in the two pictures, with spent arrows sticking out from their manes, are practically interchangeable, while the Mesopotamian hunter, drawing his bow on the stela, and the Egyptian figure supported by lions on the Gebel-el-Arak ivory (both perhaps kings?), seem even to be similarly clothed. Nor is this all. For if we require a 'least common denominator', the simplest repetitive figures in the designs from either provenance will serve the purpose of comparison. For example, the standing combatants on the obverse of the Egyptian ivory are distinguished from the ritually naked priests in the procession on the Mesopotamian vase only by the Predynastic codpieces. For the rest, both outline and musculature are practically identical.

Such parallels could very easily be multiplied, particularly where the portrayal of animals is concerned. And even when we turn to consider the half-dozen or so examples of sculpture in the round that have survived in either field, some justifiable comparison will be apparent. There is for instance the mythical beast in the Brooklyn Museum (*Ill. 19*), of which Henri Frankfort has said that it '. . . stands at the head of a long line of monsters which appear in all the great periods of Mesopotamian art and convincingly express the terror with which man realizes his helplessness in a hostile universe'. When stripped of such metaphysical associations it becomes sculpturally comparable, for example in Egypt to Narmer's alabaster ape. Similarly, if we compare the little female statuette from Khafaje (*Ill. 20*) (the only one of its sort surviving from Protoliterate times), we notice something in the forward set of the head and a

18 Sculptured alabaster vase from Warka. At the top (*right*) the leader of a procession, probably a king (head and shoulders missing), presents a basket of fruit to the goddess Innana or her priestess, identified by the two symbols behind her. In the second row nude priests bring offerings; in the bottom rows are animals and plants symbolizing two aspects of fertility

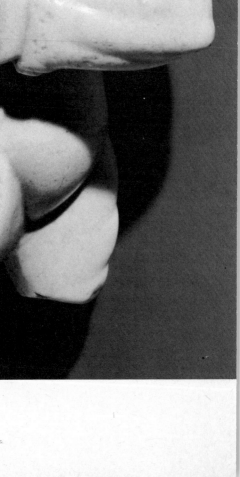

certain lack of sophisticated formality, which recalls the damaged ivory portrait of the first Egyptian Pharaoh.

In considering these parallel developments in Egypt and Mesopotamia during the final centuries of the fourth millenium B.C., and their joint contribution to the creation of world civilization, we notice the unaccountable persistence in both centres of similarities, both in artistic technique and convention, which suggest the existence of some mysterious common factor in the mentalities of two anthropologically unrelated peoples. Furthermore, mere resemblances in art become clearly related phenomena in the realms of architecture and pictographic writing; so that it is increasingly difficult to

Monster, crystalline limestone. This is the
t and perhaps the most striking of many
nstrous forms in which the Sumerians
nbolized the malevolence and hostility of
ure towards humanity

20 Statuette of a woman, from Khafaje. Being the earliest sculpture of its kind, this shows a certain naïve realism which was later lost in the greater formality and discipline of the Dynastic period

41

21 Female face in white marble from Warka. This formed part of a statue of which the greater part was made of wood. The hair would have been added in gold-leaf on bitumen and the eyes in coloured inlay

22 Reconstruction of the head shown on the previous page, as it is thought to have originally appeared. All the features were brightly coloured, and modern taste would probably prefer the incomplete to the finished version

remember that there is only the most slender and equivocal evidence for actual contacts between the two peoples at the early period.

Mesopotamian art on the other hand does show some unique developments which are purely its own. For instance there is the famous white marble head (or 'mask', as it should more properly be described) from Warka (*Ill. 21–2*), for its actual form serves to emphasize the difficulties by which Mesopotamian sculptors were faced. This must have been a life-size statue, but, owing to the scarcity of stone, it was constructed in wood, with only the exposed parts, such as hands and face, sculptured in the rarer material. The back of the head, with its elaborate coiffure, was completed in bitumen and covered with gold-leaf or copper, which extended in flat

23 Cylinder-seal impression from Khafaje. Jemdet Nasr period. A sacred herd belonging to a temple is depicted. The reed structure in the middle is a byre, and the objects projecting from it are symbols of a divinity. The engraving of these bulls shows the same freshness and vitality as appears in the larger scale animal carvings of the period

waves over the forehead. This was fixed to the stone by metal studs and no doubt appropriately engraved. The eyes, eyebrows, and parting of the hair were finally emphasized with coloured inlays. The appearance of the head with these supplementary adornments can reliably be reconstructed by analogy with later sculptures; but the mask in its surviving form has an air of simple nobility, derived solely from the sensitive modelling and luminous quality of the stone. To the modern eye, its effect is diminished by further embellishment.

Next come the carved designs on cylinder-seals, which appear for the first time in great numbers at this period (*Ill. 23*). They reflect in miniature (and may even have inspired) subjects and designs currently popular in larger scale forms of decoration which had less chance of survival. These seals were of course objects of practical utility, carried on the person and used to 'sign one's name' by rolling them on soft clay. The resulting 'impression' with its frieze-like and repetitive design, can today be more conveniently studied than the cylinder itself, on which it appears rather awkwardly in negative.

Already, during the very earliest phase of Sumerian art, quite elaborate scenes are represented in which groups of human and animal figures take part. In common with some larger carvings, such as the Warka stone vase, they give us first glimpses of Sumerian religious ritual and symbolism. We see a ceremony in progress near a temple (recognizable by the complicated reed-and-clay façade of early times), in which naked priests as usual bring offerings; or the figure of a king feeding a sacred herd of cattle. A suppliant is conducted by priests to a mother-goddess shrine, or punts himself in a boat decorated with flowers. Though their significance is often hidden from us, we are impressed by the purposeful animation of these quaint little figures. Occasionally too there are secular subjects, such as a hunting scene or a herdsman defending his flock against lions. But few of the individual motifs appear to be purely decorative, and some of the most grotesque, like 'copulating vipers' or 'serpent-headed lions', are thought to symbolize the forces of nature.

A little later, however (*Ill. 59*), the craftsmanship of the carving declines—perhaps because the spread of writing had so greatly increased the demand for seals. Insufficient care is taken to see that the traces of initial drill-holes are eliminated by secondary engraving; and a new type of design appears with a repetitive simplification of running animal-shapes, later deteriorating into frankly geometrical patterns. This has come to be known as the 'Brocade' style.

Two forms of architectural ornaments are characteristic of these times. One is applied to the outside façades of temples, which are now raised on high platforms of mud-brick. It is a form of mosaic, composed of pencil-like terracotta cones, their ends dipped in paint of various colours, which are inserted in the wet plaster of the wall-face to create a geometrical pattern (*Ill. 24*). Towards the end of the period the experiments become more ambitious, large cones of gypsum having their heads inset with coloured stone or even sheathed in bronze. A new form of interior ornament is illustrated by the attractive little temple at 'Uqair, where the walls and high

45

24 Cone mosaic from one of the engaged columns of the pillared hall at Warka. Hundreds of thousands of these coloured cones were used to create a brilliant polychrome effect. The patterns are sometimes reminiscent of textiles

...rated with painted frescoes. A band of geometrical ...eral colours serves as a base for a procession of half-... and animal figures, and their surviving lower parts ...ggest religious scenes familiar on cylinder-seals. The ...ment on the other hand, recalls both in colour and in ...rome painted pottery of the time, which had reached ...f technical accomplishment (*Ill. 25*).

...ed temples of early Sumerian times must undoubtedly ...vanced stage in the evolution of the Mesopotamian ...ge at which the Sumerian language could already

25 Painted pots from Tel Asmar. Jemdet Nasr period.
Identical colours were used in the contemporary wall-
paintings found at 'Uqair (cf. Ill. 221)

be expressed in written signs, and records of all sorts were beginning
to be kept. We are in fact approaching the period at which written
history may be said to have begun. Babylonian historians of later
times used a traditional 'Flood', as a chronological landmark in
dealing with these earliest ages. In their Dynastic lists there are kings
'before the Flood', whose names must still be legendary, since some
can be identified with epic heroes and even with gods. If then we
consider these as corresponding in time to the Predynastic kings of
Upper and Lower Egypt, their successors 'after the Flood' are probably no less authentic than the First Dynasty Pharaohs. They are

47

grouped under the names of major cities such as Kish, Erech, and Ur, which must successively have established hegemony over the whole of Sumeria.

From now onwards in the art of the two countries, the process of characteristic differentiation completes itself and is maintained almost without interruption for a matter of fifteen centuries. We must therefore look at them separately and in turn, with no more than occasional reference to comparable or contrasting idiosyncrasies. At the same time our supplementary heritage from other Near Eastern countries must be considered. Persia's contribution, though belated, will be found distinguished and important; that of other countries such as Anatolia and the Levant, commensurate only with their status as peripheral domains, in whose history lack of cultural continuity accounts for the shortcomings of an art which is mainly derivative.

In any case, the great volume of antique remains relevant to the history of art, which a dry and innocuous climate has preserved for us in the rock-cut tombs and stone buildings of Egypt, so far exceeds the corresponding legacy of other lands that it should here certainly take precedence.

PART TWO

Early Pharaohs and the Pyramid Age

Writing in 1931, the late Professor Peet gave it as his opinion that 'the general public, in so far as it is interested in Egyptian art at all, is interested in it mainly because its products are surrounded by the romance which attaches to every thing that is several thousand years old and has been dug up out of the ground'. Certainly in our own time the popular attitude towards the subject has passed through some curious vicissitudes. To the discriminating eye of the neo-classicist at the beginning of the present century, it seems to have appeared as an unintelligible archaism, rigid and immutable, obsolete while still adolescent—a sort of intractable chrysalis from which the 'perfection' of Greek art was inconsequently to emerge. By contrast, in the nineteen-twenties it was rediscovered by a group of art-critics and adopted by them (in common for instance with the work of the Benin sculptors), as a vindication of their own newly formed aesthetic convictions. It became 'the object of most enthusiastic admiration', and was acclaimed in the contemporary movement against Impressionism as 'an exemplary achievement conforming to the most modern artistic aspirations'.

In Germany during this time a great art-historian, Heinrich Schaefer, had been patiently advocating a more rational approach to the whole subject. His reasonable contention was that one should 'penetrate as deeply as possible into all the manifestations of spiritual life among the ancient Egyptians which have come down to us', in order to arouse in oneself what he called 'Egyptian thought and feeling', before attempting to interpret Egyptian art. Having done so himself very thoroughly, he was able to present his conclusions in the most enlightening form, and to provide for others a new and intelligible approach to a most rewarding subject of study. Schaefer's work was acclaimed as an indispensable contribution by British Egyptologists, one of whom went so far as to insist that 'he who has not made himself acquainted with at least its general

49

lines, is still groping about in the dark in the realm of Egyptian art: he may admire it or despise it, but he cannot really understand it'. Where Schaefer's German colleagues were concerned, however, his approach had failed to satisfy some, who insisted upon the need for a formal analysis of the actual properties inherent in the available material, without regard for the 'irrelevant' circumstances of its cultural background.

By this time the whole subject had become so controversially involved that it was excusable for some writers on the subject to content themselves with illustrating and describing a number of representative Egyptian sculptures or wall-paintings and noting the characteristics of the various periods, without going more deeply into the subject of Egyptian art as a whole. Today, the most profitable approach probably lies half-way between the two. If we are to assess the contribution of Egypt to man's total of artistic experience, we must clearly avoid judging it exclusively in terms of our own, perhaps alien, culture and endeavour first to imagine an attitude of mind which was the formative factor in the creation both of Egyptian religion and of Egyptian art. At the same time it would be quite wrong to ignore the inherent aesthetic qualities without which Egyptian sculptures and drawings would not be works of art at all. We must in fact realize that the interpretation of art in the context of cultural history should, as Frankfort has put it, 'be amplified by an analysis of its formal qualities, precisely as the interpretation of written documents in that same context is preceded by a critical examination of their linguistic qualities'.

Frankfort has also commented on the *strangeness* of Egyptian art to the modern eye—a quality which Schaefer attributes mainly to the absence in the reliefs of *perspective* as we ourselves understand it, and to the unfamiliarity of the alternative method employed in them for rendering nature. He then refers to a circumstance which might very well escape one's attention, namely that 'the use of perspective, far from being natural or common, is not even usual; its principle has been discovered only once in the whole course of human history, and that in the fifth century B.C. in Greece'. Perspective in fact is only understood today by peoples who have been directly or indirectly influenced by the principles of Greek art. If forms of art which have not been subjected to this influence should be labelled 'pre-Greek', the term must be extended not only to primitive peoples at all periods but to untaught children of our own day. The phenomena connected with *seeing* in perspective are in fact perfectly familiar to every 'pre-Greek' artist. But for purposes of drawing he rejects this view as false and resorts to a reasoned selection of his subject's known characteristics. We thus find him combining in one picture of a single object aspects of it from different viewpoints. The result is what has today come to be known as 'ideoplastic' art. For the Egyptian artist, however, one must not for a moment imagine that there is any question of a choice being made between this form of presentation and 'normal' perspective, for the latter was not yet invented. If it had been, he would have rejected it, as merely expressing a world of appearances as distinct from his own more reliable mental perception. It is for this reason that ideas rather than appearances underlie the forms which he uses.

Before returning then to our analysis of the formal qualities by which Egyptian art is distinguished, let us consider for a moment the wider subject of its purpose and *raison d'être*. Here we shall immediately be confronted by the central fact of its intimate and almost exclusive association with Egyptian religious beliefs. From the earliest times Egyptian art had no serious purpose unconnected with religion—a circumstance which becomes less surprising when one remembers the magnitude of the part which religion played in Egyptian life generally, among a people incapable of distinguishing between religious and political thought. And here is another sense in which the label 'pre-Greek' could be applied to Egyptian attitudes of mind. For every aspect of their public and private lives was seen by them against a pattern of religious beliefs or practices, which totally excluded what might be called the 'lay outlook'. The classical separation of religious authority from civic administration, or the still later distinction between Church and State would have been incomprehensible in Dynastic Egypt.

To turn to the actual character of Egyptian religion, we must remember first its preoccupation with monarchy as the earthly manifestation of divine power and with the prolongation of life after death; the symbolism of its complicated mythology and ritual conventions which permeated the whole fabric of daily life. Its main principles and the imagery by which they were expressed, were already stabilized during the Fourth Dynasty, but the centuries that followed saw a long process of elaboration. For Egyptian religious ideas did not so much grow as accumulate. As Cyril Aldred has said—'Little was ever rejected by this conservative people, and it is probable that Egyptian religion could mean all things to all men from philosophical ideas for the educated few in an age of culture, to a mere superstition for the unquestioning masses at a period of decline.'

The function of Egyptian art was to express religious abstractions in a comprehensible form, to create for religious purposes lasting memorials of persons and events, and to provide appropriate settings for religious rituals. The nature of this work implied a restrictive discipline for the artist himself, and it is him whom we must next consider. We shall observe his lack of individual status and the limitations imposed on him by convention to the exclusion of actual style, as well as the creative ingenuity which enabled him to overcome such disabilities; and we shall be able to study in the solution which he reached, some interesting characteristics reflecting the peculiar environment in which he lived.

We have mentioned earlier how certain prehistoric figurines can be identified as 'cult-objects'. Logically there is no reason why the same term should not be applied to the bulk of Egyptian statuary. Being predominantly monumental in intent, it has a well-defined function relating to a religious cult, and the purpose of the cult is a memorial one—that is, it is aimed at perpetuating the memory (and thereby the existence) of human personality. At first this cult seems

→

26 Statuette of King Pepy I, six inches high, in green slate, with inlaid eyes. This is the earliest *ex voto* statue showing a king kneeling to make a libation. Unlike the funerary cult-statues, it is largely freed from the formal inhibitions of stone-carving and shows a surprising naturalism

to have been associated exclusively with royalty. It was in fact concerned with what has been called 'the grandiose paradox of sacred kingship'; not, at first, with *divine* kingship, since belief in the *ex officio* divinity of kings seems to have been a secondary development; but with the prolongation of a cycle of existence which would otherwise end in death. Starting as a royal prerogative, the privileges of the cult were afterwards extended to the royal family, and later again, with diminishing discrimination to their associates and dependents; so that the usage could be adapted to universal belief in survival and the statuary to the funerary requirements of private people (*Ill. 27*). It is a little surprising to remind oneself that the Egyptian artist could, in this way, fairly be described as a 'monumental mason', with little reservation regarding the connotation which modern usage has given to the term. The proper setting for his work was in association with a tomb; and this in fact is where it is for the most part found.

The function of a mortuary statue within the cult was that of a human image, assuming or supplementing the identity of the embalmed corpse in perpetuity. For this purpose it had to be a portrait of a sort which would avoid any suggestion of mortal frailty or the ephemeral nature of human life. It therefore had to be rendered without emphasis on the organic aspect of the original, and invested with a static quality compatible with the 'timelessness' of its purpose. The Egyptian sculptors, with their incomparable skill, not only encompassed abstractions such as these, but at the same time succeeded in achieving a 'likeness'—not, in all probability, a literal resemblance, which would have involved them in irrelevant considerations such as character and mood, but the distinctive insignia of the essential individuality. Actual resemblance was in fact a

→

27 Pair-statue of Mykerinus and his Queen. The first of its kind to be made, it set a fashion among people of less exalted rank for having themselves portrayed supported by or even embracing their wives. In a royal monument of this sort, the identical treatment of the two figures suggests that the statue's secondary purpose was to perpetuate some more human aspects of the King's earthly existence

secondary consideration, for the identity of the statue could be even less equivocally established by a ritual process of 'naming'. And herein lies the significance of inscriptions on these statues, incorporating the name of the deceased, for if a statue came to be appropriated to the use of a second person, a change in the written title could render the facial evidence invalid. A practice tending towards the reverse extreme is illustrated by the so-called 'reserve heads' from the royal workshops of the Fourth Dynasty at Giza, which were placed in the actual burial-chamber (*Ill. 31*). They seem to have had the function of supernumerary portraits, added as a precaution against the destruction or defacement of the body itself. The mortuary statue also, for precautionary reasons, could be duplicated: as many as fifty were found in the great Fifth Dynasty *mastaba* of Khnum-baf.

In this funerary sculpture one already begins to detect signs of a unique and characteristic approach to aesthetic problems, which is in fact essentially Egyptian. Attempts made in the past to analyse this have almost invariably led to the conclusion that the Egyptian artist must have been psychologically influenced to a very great extent by his physical environment. The dependable constancy of the climate and the predictable rhythm of the Nile's seasonal flooding were for him reassuring certainties in a preordained way of life. Then there was the geographical isolation of the country within its natural frontiers. Protected along its sides by deserts and easily defensible, it was at the same time insulated from the great migratory movements which disturbed the neighbouring lands of the Near East. This seems to have induced in the Egyptians generally a sense of security and permanence, and in the artist (rather curiously) a preoccupation with every manifestation of a present existence, in which the past and the future seemed somehow to be integrated. In his imagination the actual concept of death did not exist. As the

→

28 Rahotep and Nofret. An unusually well-preserved example of the painted stone statue, giving a good idea of the original colouring; the eyes are inlaid with crystal. These figures are the work of the same school as the 'reserve heads' (*Ill. 31*)

29 (*above*) Statue of Herniunu, the vizier and architect to King Cheops. This famous statue stands apart from traditional Egyptian sculpture and sets its own standards. It appears not to have been painted, so that the extreme subtlety of the modelling is not obscured. No attempt has been made to disguise the symptoms of advancing age, but the figure gives an impression of dignity and wisdom. This statue is probably as near to being a 'portrait', in the modern sense, as Egyptian art ever got

Opposite: 30 (*left*) Head of Prince Ankh-kaf; 31 (*right*) A 'reserve head' of the daughter-in-law of Cheops; one of a pair from Sakkara

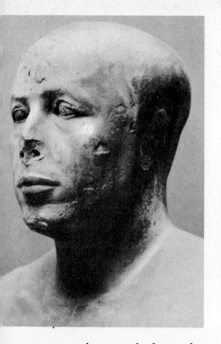 

sun was reborn each day and Osiris each year, so for the Egyptian death was simply the night before the triumphant passage to ever-lasting day.

Another geographical consideration was the Egyptian's official conception of his country as a dual entity. Unless we agree with Frankfort, who considers this merely a 'mode of thought which conceived totality as an equilibrium of opposites' and had no basis in fact after the unification of the country by Menes, we must look for distinctive traits in the art of the 'Two Lands'. In fact, from what little we know of the Delta it appears to have differed from Upper Egypt, not only in climate and economy, but in the character of its inhabitants, who had to some extent assimilated their habits of thought to those of their Asiatic neighbours. Where their art is concerned, one may perhaps take their use of limestone in preference to the austerities of southern granite, as a symbol of their aesthetic taste (*Ill. 33*). In fact it showed symptoms of instinctive naturalism in contrast to the conceptual formalism of Upper Egypt.

Two sculptures in contrasting materials. 32 (*left*) Granite head from Sakkara; 33 (*right*) Limestone head of Mykerinus from Giza. The different materials—extremely hard in the one case, easy to work in the other—had much to do with the development of regional styles in the areas where they were predominantly used. An unusual feature in the Mykerinus head is the representation of the locks of hair at the edge of the wig-cover

Yet it is to the artists of the Upper Nile Valley that we must attribute almost all the primary characteristics of Old Kingdom art, as we know it in its most distinctive form. And here all art-historians seem agreed on the psychological reaction of these people to certain abstract qualities in their peculiar environment. For the Upper Egyptian there were no circular horizons. The shape of his immediate world was manifestly rectilinear; confined between the ruthless parallels of the escarpment, which separates the cultivated valley from the high desert on either side. A third dimension was provided by the floor of the valley itself and by the sky, which the Egyptian imagination conceived as a rigid canopy suspended on invisible uprights. Some critics have attributed to this Egyptian obsession with the *prismatic* aspect of his world, the preference which he shows for basically cubic forms in his sculpture. No one could fail to notice how nearly his most typical product conforms to an imaginary cube, and it is not fashionable to explain this peculiarity by reference to methods of quarrying stone or to the fact that such sculptures were usually intended as mere units in the design of a strictly rectilinear building. It is considered rather to depend on a space-conception which satisfies his aesthetic predilections. The device which he adopts is first to consider the two profiles of his subject independently. They are then amalgamated into a three-dimensional form in which reminiscences of the original cube are purposely retained. Square thrones or plinths further emphasize the basic geometrical shape. By the same token it has been observed that, where tomb-paintings are concerned, he prefers a self-contained rectilinear treatment for each separate wall and an unrelated ceiling, like the 'canopy' of the sky. All this has been associated with the Egyptian's curious, psychological sense of *confinement*—a sort of 'claustrophilia' (as Aldred expressively calls it), which disposes him towards the 'comfort' of a

→

34 King Khephren. This statue, one of over a hundred that stood in the pyramid complex of Khephren at Giza, was to be a model for all funerary statues of the future. The monumental pose, the attitude of the hands—the right probably holding a sceptre—and the formalized symmetry of the features make it a perfect symbol of divine royalty

final resting-place in the angular obscurity of a stone sarcophagus or rock-cut tomb. It is an interesting theory and, if it accounts indirectly for the dignity of Upper Egyptian art, it also helps to explain some of its limitations.

It is perhaps worth pointing out that in all this we have been considering Egyptian artists collectively. As individuals they can hardly be said to have existed and their personal predilections were of no account. Their works were not intended for the delectation or edification of a public whose approbation might flatter or profit their authors: indeed they were seldom even intended to be *seen*. As repositories of superhuman force, they were destined to remain forever hidden from the profanity of human sight in shrines and tomb-chambers. The artists themselves were in fact generally anonymous: not individual contributors to a fabric of creative production, but simple artisans engaged in a hereditary calling. What amazes us today is the intuitive sensibility which enabled these nameless craftsmen to devise an aesthetic means of expressing prescribed abstractions, and to invest this device with an emotional appeal which is as valid today as it must have been in their own time. Yet the appeal is no more than a by-product of the practical achievement. For however we choose to label or interpret the impulses contributing to accomplishment, the simple fact remains that during the reigns of the earliest Egyptian Pharaohs, these great masters perfected a system of presenting organic subjects such as men and animals in a manner so splendidly convincing and aesthetically satisfying that it was accepted wholesale by later generations and considered beyond criticism. Let us now consider their work in greater detail.

The first two Egyptian dynasties are usually referred to as the 'Archaic period', and it is one from which unfortunately very few works of art have survived. One conspicuous exception is the Narmer palette (*Ill. 14*), on which we have already seen the figures of 'Menes', wearing alternately the crowns of the Southern and Northern Kingdoms, and the device of united 'lions', whose symbolism we can hardly doubt. Yet there is reason to think that the political rivalry between the 'Two Lands' continued intermittently

35 Statue (restored) of King Kha-Sekhem. The King wears the white crown of the south. This statue already shows the typical Egyptian characteristic of approximating to a cubic form. The position of the left arm, which brings both hands on to the same side, is awkward and was seldom repeated

until the end of the Second Dynasty, when a more lasting unity was achieved under a king called Kha-Sekhem, whose portrait has survived in the form of two funerary statues (*Ill. 35*). This general situation seems to be reflected in the location of the earliest royal tombs. Some were found at Abydos in Upper Egypt where, either in respect for family traditions or because the Kingdom was once more divided, certain southern kings appear to have had themselves buried. At Memphis however, a site conveniently intermediate between the Delta and Upper Egypt, the vast royal cemetery was also already in use; and recent excavations have revealed, near Sakkara, First Dynasty tombs with obviously regal attributes. One of these seems to combine two different grave-forms—the tumulus-shaped structure characteristic of the south and the panelled brick *mastaba* more typical of Lower Egypt. This one was the tomb of a queen, who

65

36 Ivory label from a pair of sandals, showing King Udimu striking down an Asiatic adversary. His symbolic gesture is the same as that on the Narmer palette (*Ill. 14*) and it continued to be repeated throughout the history of Egyptian art

appears to have died in the reign of Udimu, fifth king of the First Dynasty. (His figure also appears on an ivory plaque in the British Museum (*Ill. 36*)—one of the few small monuments to have survived from the Archaic period—where he is depicted in the now classical attitude of slaying an enemy, in this case recognizable as an Asiatic, which perhaps suggests some conquest beyond the combined frontiers of the 'Two Lands'.)

These *mastaba* tombs were rectangular brick structures with many internal compartments built over the actual subterranean burial-chamber. Their façades were decorated with a complicated arrangement of buttresses and recesses—an architectural device whose unmistakably Mesopotamian character has been accepted by some archaeologists as the first considerable evidence for contact between the two countries. Others suppose that it was the elaboration of such buildings by the addition of superimposed upper storeys on a diminishing scale, which developed logically into the 'Step Pyramid' built by Zoser, the first king of the Third Dynasty.

King Zoser's architect, Im-hetep, is traditionally credited with the invention of stone masonry. Certainly the extensive complex of elegant buildings surrounding Zoser's tomb at Sakkara, bear witness

37 Relief from the tomb of Ti, Sakkara. On the right men
with harpoons are hunting hippopotamus, which swim in
the river. At the top of the composition birds are trying to
protect their young in the nests. Ti stands in a small skiff
watching. The vertical lines in the background are a stylized
representation of papyrus reeds growing along the banks of
the Nile

to his remarkable ingenuity, not only in rendering effectively in limestone forms peculiar to the brick-buildings of earlier times, but in converting organic shapes into attractively stylized ornament (*Ill. 224*). His treatment of ceilings, for example, reflecting the closely set, circular wooden rafters of another age, and his stone columns with their vertical reeding, resembling bundles of papyrus stalks, and their 'pendant-leaf' capitals, show evidence of a sensitive taste in design which has no parallel in later times. One indeed wishes that more examples had survived of the sculpture which went with it. Unfortunately we have hardly more than a set of rather un-illuminating wall-reliefs (*Ill. 42*) and one portrait-statue (*Ill. 38*), which was found still in place in the *serdab* chamber. In spite of the damaged condition in which it has survived, one can already recognize in this figure the fully developed attributes of the Old Kingdom mortuary sculpture.

The Old Kingdom properly begins with the Third Dynasty, but its full characteristics do not become apparent until the Fourth. This was the age of the great pyramid-builders—an age of formalism, in which all early symptoms of individuality or naturalism were swept away, to be replaced by a rigid code of authoritarian convention. Once the intellectual impact of these influential autocrats had taken effect, the imagery of Egyptian art crystallized in a definitive form (*Ill. 34*). 'Deviationism' was forsworn for a thousand years.

So let us finally turn our attention from actual statuary of the Old Kingdom to the sculptured reliefs and paintings, which decorate the walls, not only of mortuary temples, but of the tombs of private individuals. One of the earliest examples of the latter is the Third Dynasty tomb of the royal scribe, Hesy-ra (*Ill. 39*). The famous

$\rightarrow$

38 Statue of King Zoser. This statue, which was much damaged when its inlaid eyes were at some time prized out of its head, achieves a powerfully monumental effect from its formal adaption to the cubic simplicity of the throne upon which it sits. In the dark *serdab* chamber of the tomb it could only be seen through two holes pierced in the front wall. It is the oldest life-sized mortuary statue and has the King's name incised on the base

wooden panels in which he is portrayed with such fine craftsmanship stand facing a long frieze, depicting, not as yet actual scenes,
but groups of his possessions and the everyday utensils of his life.
Next, dating from the Fourth Dynasty (when decoration was more
often austerely restricted), there are the paintings in the tomb of
Ranofer at Meidum, where he also is pictured as a living man, this
time regarding a sequence of little scenes relating to his earthly
existence. (They are still arranged with considerable simplicity in
horizontal sequences or 'registers' around the 'false door' through
which, in tombs of his time, the dead was supposed to communicate
with the living.) These two arrangements form a prelude to the
fully developed reliefs of the Sakkara tombs (*Ill. 43*) where the
figure of the occupant, distinguished by his disproportionate size,
dominates a series of busy and naturalistic episodes and situations,
typifying his normal life. There are agricultural scenes in which
labourers are harvesting or attending to animals; servants and scribes
assembling the produce or revenues of his estate; boating scenes or
hunting expeditions among the birds and animals of the marshes. In
all these the dead man seems specifically to be portrayed, not as
participating in such activities or even supervising them, but merely
as *watching* them. Mrs Frankfort takes this to mean that the function
of the reliefs is to appease his assumed nostalgia. What we see is the
'image of the man-in-death, watching life's familiar manifestations'.

Of reliefs in royal mortuary temples we have so far mentioned
only a single group, from a building annexed to Zoser's tomb at
Sakkara. These carvings depicted the King taking part in a ceremonial race (*Ill. 42*). During the remainder of the Third Dynasty the
subject of such reliefs continued to be predominantly religious and

→

39 Wooden panel from the tomb of Hesy-ra, Sakkara.
This relief, dating from the reign of Zoser, already embodies
all the elements of the stylistic formula rigidly adhered to
in later times. It is characteristic of the 'pre-Greek' approach
to art, where superficial appearances are discarded in favour
of mentally perceived realities. Aspects of the subject from
different viewpoints are combined in the composition of a
picture, whose function is that of a meaningful ideogram

40 Reliefs from the tomb of Mereruka. This is a large private (i.e. non-royal) tomb, containing painted limestone-reliefs notable for their bold execution and originality of composition. They show mostly scenes from rural life. In the top

row asses are being loaded with panniers and driven forward by sticks. In the bottom row (*right*) corn is being cut and (*centre*) tied up into bundles. The hieroglyphics represent the playful banter of the workers

73

41 Relief of the god Geb from the Zoser shrine, Heliopolis. The face is drawn in the convention noted earlier, with intricate archaic detail in the carving of the wig, beard, and necklace, as well as in the slender hieroglyphs

was often associated with the cult of the sun-god, Ra. In the Fourth, mortuary reliefs seem hardly to have featured at all, perhaps because the tremendous austerity of granite temples and the ponderous monumentality of their statuary made surface ornament seem incongruously trivial. But thereafter they begin to reappear, and in the Fifth Dynasty there are, for instance, the beautiful sculptures from the funerary temple of Sahure, to illustrate the variety of subjects which were now considered suitable. They also serve to show some distinctive features of *royal* reliefs, as opposed to those in private tombs.

If we remember at what an early stage the divinity of the living Pharaoh became a primary article of Egyptian religious belief, a

74

42 Relief of King Zoser, from a false door-panel (Sakkara). The King is taking part in a ritual race. He carries a flail and wears the crown of Upper Egypt. The carving is in very low relief, but small modulations of the surface are enough to suggest bone structure

moment's reflection will show that the function of the
must differ radically from that of pictures in the tom
mortals. The nostalgic confrontation of the dead ma
amenities of human existence, in the case of a god, wou
paradoxical. Instead of 'watching', then, the figure c
participates in and even directs the events pictured; and
feeling that the sculptures themselves have once more
purely monumental function. The perpetuation of the Kin

76

43 Relief from the tomb of Ptah-hotep at Sakkara. The dead man, shown as usual on a much larger scale than the common people, stretches out his hand to receive the King's gifts. We also see the produce of the fields, musicians playing and, at the top, craftsmen at work. These and other everyday scenes, familiar to him during his life on earth, are depicted in order to appease the nostalgic loneliness of his tomb

in the hereafter is not for a moment in doubt; but there are other more ephemeral attributes of royalty, such as the dignity of material accomplishment or the attainment of worldly fame (as well as some purely human needs such as family affection), whose survival must be ensured.

The total of reliefs from both these classes of building, including the astonishingly beautiful carvings from the tomb of Ti at Sakkara (*Ill. 37*), constitute a major contribution of the Old Kingdom to the world's art-treasures. The delicate line-drawing and masterful precision of their carving have no equal in later periods. After the end of the Fourth Dynasty the armies of craftsmen employed on the grandiose projects of the pyramid-builders, rendered temporarily idle by their completion, made their services available to a wider and less discriminating class of patrons, and by the Sixth, a process of obvious vulgarization has begun. Carving in deep relief is an innovation, and one which obviously allows greater latitude for imperfect craftsmanship. Nevertheless, in royal circles at least, the exacting standards of earlier days are maintained until the end of the Old Kingdom. The reliefs from the funerary temple of Pepy II bear comparison with the best carving of the era.

With such a picture in mind, of Egypt during the period of the Old Kingdom—a land united under the rule of a single divine king, and a people whose precocious mentality had already evolved a formal system of abstract expression—we must now turn to Mesopotamia. We shall find ourselves faced with many contrasts and some curious complexities which may once more be attributed as much to physical environment as to the racial characteristics of the people with whom we are dealing.

PART THREE

Creative Genius in Mesopotamia and a Reflection in Anatolia

SUMER AND AKKAD

We find ourselves once more in the early centuries of the third millennium B.C., and in the great alluvial basin at the head of the Persian Gulf. Sumerian civilization is now in full flower. But this is no single united Kingdom. It is a pattern of city-states, each of them at first a primitive democracy ruled by a council of leading citizens. Individual leaders were only chosen to deal with temporary emergencies, though it was doubtless the prolongation of such crises which eventually gave them a more permanent status. Even then, the titles attributed to them were in themselves equivocal. *Ensi* ('city-governor') alternated with *lugal* ('king'), when the city extended its dominion by conquest. But even *lugal* had no more pretentious meaning than 'great man', and was used by tradition in certain cities regardless of their station in preference to *ensi* or other titles—(rather as the head of a modern college may be 'president', 'master', 'warden', etc.). Kings were not thought of as gods until Akkadian times, and then only certain individuals acquired this distinction. These 'kings' in fact had a rather modest conception of themselves as political and religious 'leaders' of their small States; and when later large parts of the country tended to become temporarily united under a single ruler, he became merely 'Shepherd of the Black-headed People', i.e. the Sumerians.

Dynasties of Sumerian kings ruling in cities such as Ur, Erech, or Kish, were listed by Babylonian scribes of later times, and gained reality in our own generation when archaeologists found their names mentioned in inscriptions associated with tombs and monuments. It is for this reason that the true Sumerian period is usually known as Early Dynastic.

Under this régime, great advances were made in cultural evolution. Cities were fortified and adorned with public buildings; law-codes

79

were drawn up; canals were dug to irrigate the land and improve communications by boat; armies were equipped and troops trained for the first time to move in orderly formation, victories were celebrated and treaties ratified. As a result, when one comes to study the total of art-objects surviving from this period one finds that a fair number of them have a monumental function, commemorating purely secular events such as military conquests, the completion of a building, or opening of a canal. These take the form of stone stelae sculptured in relief or carved stone plaques. But the remainder, which constitute a far greater majority, are made to serve obvious religious purposes of one sort or another; and included in this category are all statues of whatever material, carved or constructed in the round, for these are invariably intended for a place in the sanctuary of a temple. Purely decorative designs without either commemorative or religious purpose are rarest of all (though strangely enough, during the first of the three phases into which archaeology has divided the Early Dynastic period, these include cylinder-seals, whose designers had temporarily become preoccupied with mere pattern).

In any approach to the nature and origins of Sumerian religion, the first factor to note is as usual the influence of environment; the effects of geological and climatic conditions on contemporary superstitions and beliefs. Like the Egyptians, the inhabitants of the Tigris and Euphrates valleys were above all dependent for their livelihood on river water. But the Sumerians had also to rely on irrigation by means of canals; and to an almost equal extent, they depended on the precarious comfort of the spring rains, whose failure could bring famine and disaster. For five months in the summer the Mesopotamian climate creates a purgatory of heat and desiccation, during which man's hope of survival is directly dependent on the products of his own industry during the winter and spring. There is no reason to think that conditions differed greatly in the third millennium B.C. Beasts of prey, poisonous insects, and disease were other dangers against which a Sumerian was compelled to guard himself; so that in the end, all his will-power and ingenuity were continually pitted against hostile and potentially destructive elements in nature. In

44 Cylinder-seal from Ur, second Early Dynastic period. Two bulls couchant on either side of a triple plant and protected by human figures from attacking eagles, bulls, stag, and ibex underneath

these circumstances success and prosperity naturally came to be identified with the principle of fertility, a blessing to which the Sumerian anxiously aspired through prayer, as well as by practical contrivance. But it is also hardly surprising if, from a religious point of view, he is found to conceive himself as 'subject without appeal to the acts of distant and fearful divinities whom he serves but cannot love'.

All this is perfectly expressed in Sumerian religious practices, and even more so in the fabric of contemporary mythology. For it must be remembered that any definition which we ourselves may formulate of the Mesopotamian attitude towards nature and man's precarious destiny, is based on abstractions beyond the capacity of Sumerian introspection. Myths were the natural remedy for this short-coming. They served as a tangible garment of uncomplicated imagery in which to clothe abstract conclusions and to perpetuate the revelations of thought or experience. The philosophic convictions and beliefs of an entire people are embodied in Sumerian mythology.

81

45 Im-dugud, the benevolent lion-headed eagle of Sumerian myth, appears in charge of two stags in a huge copper-relief, forty-two inches high, which ornamented a Sumerian temple at Al 'Ubaid

This is the reason why the pictorial presentation of mythical figures and events provides the subject of so much Sumerian art. Information from this source alone would indeed have sufficed to familiarize us with them, even if they had not meanwhile been introduced to us in literary form. The 'Bull of Heaven', for instance, whose fiery breath burns up the crops (*Ill. 44*), is a figure easy to identify, and it requires little imagination to see in the intervention of the ponderous lion-headed eagle, Im-dugud, whose wings shroud the heavens in dark clouds (*Ill. 45*), the image of a benevolent rainstorm bringing an end to a prolonged drought. Then also there is the pantheon of Sumerian deities, with its several trinities including figures like Tammuz (the 'dying-god' of *The Golden Bough*) who descends 'beneath the mountain' when vegetation succumbs to the heat and desiccation of the summer, and must be resurrected in the spring for his symbolic marriage with Inanna, the 'earth-mother', in order to ensure the fertility of crops and herds.

Some of these myths were not only recorded in writing and depicted by artists, but ceremonially recited during appropriate

celebrations; and in certain cases, as though the virtue of the myth itself could be made more effective by repetition, they were actually dramatized. In Sumer, the great festivals which marked successive stages in the natural progress of the seasons provided occasions for these performances and culminated in the fertility ritual associated with the New Year. This was the *hieros gamos*—the 'holy-marriage' between god and goddess, whose symbolism was enacted on the raised sanctuary of the *ziggurat* temple, the male role being played by the King himself.

The actual sources from which surviving works of art are derived throw further light on the character of Sumerian religion. In Egypt, more than fifty per cent of extant sculptures and paintings have their origin in tombs or are associated in some way with funerary monuments. All bear witness directly or indirectly to the Egyptian belief in man's survival after death. Sumerian philosophy, in contrast to Egyptian, seems reluctantly to accept the finite character of his existence. A large part, for instance, of the famous Gilgamesh epic is concerned with the great hero's quest for the secret of

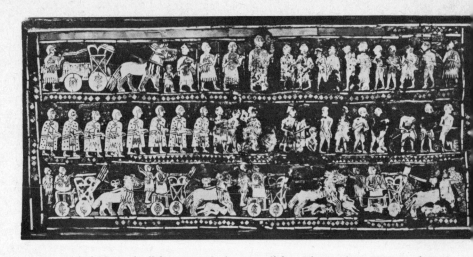

46 'Inlaid Standard' from Ur. The 'war panel' face. The two lower registers depict a battle: Sumerian infantry in metal helmets, cloaks, and fleece kilts; four-wheeled chariots drawn by four wild asses. In the top register the King, taller than his men, descends from his chariot to inspect captives

immortality; and one notices how, when faced with ultimate failure, he resigns himself to the conclusion that 'when the gods created man they let death be his share, and life withheld in their own hands'. For the Sumerians in fact, a central preoccupation was with the task of securing a reliable pattern of existence in the shadow of their own mortality; and it was for this reason that their religious beliefs focused themselves on the miracles of procreation and the seasonal resurrection of natural fecundity. As for honouring the dead or providing for their life in the hereafter, the evidence on this subject is surprisingly scarce. For out of a total of some six hundred kings who must have ruled in Mesopotamia up to the final fall of Babylon and Nineveh, the tombs of no more than half a dozen have been found; and, with the exception of the First Dynasty tombs at Ur, whose 'royalty' is controversial, all had been plundered in antiquity.

Nevertheless, it is from the treasures in the so-called 'Royal Cemetery' at Ur that we obtain a first impression of Sumerian taste

84

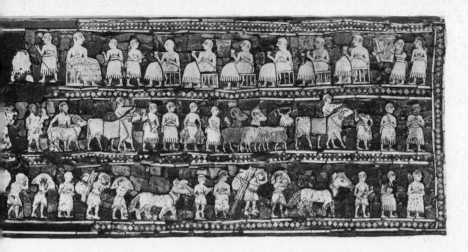

47 The reverse side of the 'Standard', showing the victory feast. In the top register the King and his officers are seated drinking. In the two lower registers booty, including captured teams of asses, is paraded before them. The purpose of this 'Standard' is not known

in design and the rich versatility of Mesopotamian craftsmanship. Archaic inscriptions found in the tombs themselves do not prove the occupants kings and queens; they may also have been priests and priestesses, sacrificed after playing some role in the annual fertility rite. However this may be, they were buried amid an elaborate and valuable profusion of tomb-furniture, and accompanied to the grave by richly dressed attendants, guards, and chariots. Among the treasures recovered from these tombs, there are individual works of great interest. One of these at least seems to be imagery serving a purely commemorative purpose. It is the so-called 'Standard'—a double-sided panel on which tiny figures in shell or mother-of-pearl are inlaid in bitumen against a mosaic of lapis-lazuli, and complicated events are thus depicted in horizontal sequences or registers within borders of similar materials. The scene shown on one side (*Ill. 46*) is a battle with chariots and infantry engaged, and on the other (*Ill. 47*) a feast is in progress at which a victory is being celebrated, while various forms of booty are paraded before the participants. In

85

48. Carved relief from Khafaje, showing a feast in progress. The subject had become so rigidly standardized that a gap in the bottom left-hand corner is quite satisfactorily filled by a fragment from a similar plaque found at Ur

each scene the figure of a king is recognizable by its slightly exaggerated size. As an introduction to the dress, appearance, and behaviour of the Sumerians, this is a remarkably revealing document. It also serves well to illustrate some idiosyncrasies obviously though inexplicably common to both Sumerian and Egyptian drawing, such as confusion of aspects (front-face and profile combined), and multiplication by the *échelon* method (for example the chariot horses).

Other works in this category were more conventionally carved in stone. And 'conventionally' is here perhaps a suitable word: for square plaques bearing a simplified version of the battle-and-feast scene seem to have been duplicated with such precision that, for instance, one such object found at Khafaje, with half of the lower

49 Stela of Urnanshe from Telloh. A Sumerian commemorative relief. Urnan-she, watched by his family, brings earth to make the first brick of a new temple and (*below*) celebrates its completion

register missing, could be completed by the addition of a fragment carved at Ur, a hundred miles away (*Ill. 48*). If the Ur 'Standard' commemorated a specific victory, pictures such as these are probably no more than a polite formality.

By contrast with the anonymity of these scenes, there is a similar plaque, carved by Urnanshe, a ruler of Lagash, to celebrate his construction of a new temple (*Ill. 49*). His own figure and those of his family are here drawn rather crudely, but they are covered with incised hieroglyphs recording their names, almost to the point of obscuring the design. For a work showing greater aesthetic consideration in its design, one must turn to a sculpture of more general public significance. The stela of Eannatum, also from Telloh (Lagash) (*Ill. 50*), has been reconstructed from pitifully few

87

50 Both sides of fragment Eannatum's stela of victo from Telloh. *Left:* The g Ningirsu entangles the Kir enemies in a symbolic n *Right:* Eannatum hims King of Lagash, leads his p lanx into battle and drives own chariot

fragments: but it can be reliably identified as a boundary-stone, set up after a battle to record a contractual agreement between victor and vanquished. Here, in addition to the purely monumental and commemorative function of the sculpture, the religious aspect of the event is emphasized. The battle is in fact over and the Sumerian phalanx has resumed its orderly formation: but the figure of the king, 'first among equals', is hardly distinguishable from his troops. It is to the giant figure of the god Ningirsu that attention is drawn, and his responsibility for victory is thus piously acknowledged. It is he who holds the King's enemies in a symbolical net. Sculpturally these fragments give a rare glimpse of Sumerian relief-carving at its best. A group of rather different reliefs, usually carved in hard green stone with coloured inlay, date from the second phase of the Early Dynastic period (*Ill. 51*). Their subjects are mostly secular and have a curiously exotic character. Indeed, the appearance in one of them of an Indian-humped bull (zebu) led at first to the erroneous impression that they were of foreign origin.

The inlay technique of the Ur 'Standard' is also applied to the decoration of major figures in the round from the same source. Conspicuously beautiful are the wooden harps with their animal figureheads and ornamental panels; perhaps most striking of all being the gold bull's head in *Ill. 52*. Both design and materials have been so skilfully adapted to the creation of this remarkable emblem that, as Sir Leonard Woolley once remarked, admiration blinds one to the incongruity of a bull wearing a beard. The grotesque animal figures of the inlaid panel make an interesting contrast. The gold and lapis goat in *Ill. 57*, probably used as a support for a bowl of incense, clearly has more than mere decorative significance. For the Sumerians the goat was the personification of virility; and this figure, with the emblems of vegetation among which its horns are thrust, must symbolize dual aspects of fertility, animal and vegetable. There is a contemporary hymn in which Tammuz himself is apostrophized as 'Leading Goat of the Land'. Then there is the straightforward jewellers' and goldsmiths' work: the court head-dresses

51 Carved steatite vase from Khafaje. The symbolism of the design seems once more to emphasize the natural hazards of a herdsman's life in Mesopotamia. One animal depicted is a humped bull of the Indian zebu breed, which is not native to Mesopotamia; but the human figure is unmistakably Sumerian

with their diadems of willow or beech-leaves, wrought in gold and crests of metal flowers (*Ill. 54*). Museum reconstructions of these complex ornaments are impressive: but the position chosen for the diadem—almost entirely obscuring the forehead—has always appeared unconvincing and today is subject to increasing doubt. The most common form of Sumerian coiffure consists of a chignon partly concealed by a heavy plait in the form of a tiara. It is more probable that the diadem lay over this plait, which would explain its excessive length, for instance in the case of 'Queen Shubad'. Some of the most charming objects of all are the chaste and simply fluted vases of gold (*Ill. 55*); and, rivalling them, the ceremonial knives with their studded lapis hafts and sheaths of golden filigree (*Ill. 56*), products of craftsmanship unexcelled in later times. Some ceremonial treasures have the extra interest that their purpose is illustrated

$\rightarrow$

52 Gold bull's head, from a lyre, found at Ur. Gold-leaf over a wooden core; hair and beard of lapis-lazuli. This head ornamented the sound-box of the lyre; its perfection of design makes the beard appear hardly incongruous

53 Golden wig-helmet of Mes-kalam-shar from Ur: two views, posed on a plaster model. Features such as the ears are modelled in relief and the details engraved. When worn, the inside of the helmet was lined with cloth, held in place through holes along the lower edge. (Compare the King's helmet in *Ill. 50*)

in actual pictures. In the Eannatum stela for instance, the king is seen to be wearing a more practical counterpart of the golden wig-helmet from the tomb of Mes-kalam-shar (*Ill. 53*). The rein-ring in *Ill. 58* surmounted by an ass, beautifully modelled in an alloy of gold and silver, appears on chariot-shafts in the 'Standard' battle scene.

Some of the finest relief-carving of the Early Dynastic period is to be found on cylinder-seals. In its earlier phase, subject-matter had been subordinated to pattern. The designs were composed of motifs, sometimes still just recognizable as moving files of animals, but more often purely ornamental, woven together into a continuous frieze and forming a pattern of unvarying density. In the second phase there was a sudden renewal of interest in the pictorial possibilities of the designs; and no lack of subjects was found among the fantastic imagery of Sumerian mythology (*Ill. 60, 61*). Elaborate scenes, in

54 Head-dress of a woman, from Ur. This consists of leaves and flowers made in gold in a setting of semi-precious stones such as carnelian. We cannot be certain how it was meant to be worn; possibly the ornamental wreath should be raised clear of the forehead

which beasts, humans, and imaginary oddities play conventional roles, contract themselves into formal designs by counterpoise and enlacement of the figures, and, where space-filling is required, isolated symbols are interposed between them. Once more a continuous pattern of unvarying density is thus devised.

The detailed meaning of these seal-pictures is not always clear. The symbolism is often obscure, and we are frequently hampered by ignorance of the most commonplace mythological concepts. Nevertheless, the total broad significance of some continually recurring figures can be understood and main themes guessed at. The most universal motif is conflict—usually between lions and the mythical protectors of flocks and herds which they have attacked. Two figures—a 'naked hero' and a 'bull-man'—appear with great frequency as protectors and have often been identified with the

93

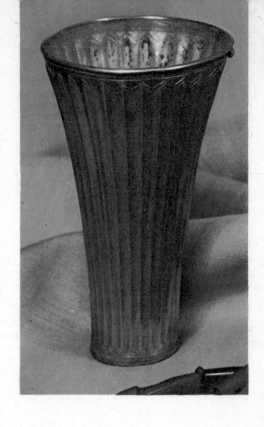

55 (*above*) Gold vase from Ur; the sides are fluted; round the top and bottom is a herringbone pattern and double zig-zag

56 (*left*) Gold dagger from Ur; the blade is of gold with central rib; the hilt, of wood plated with silver and gold-studded, has a gold guard, studded with gold nails

57 (*right*) 'The Ram caught in the thicket' from Ur. An offering-stand of gold, silver, and lapis-lazuli over a wooden core in the form of a goat (the shoulders supported some form of receptacle). The powerful beast thrusting its horns among the emblems of vegetation symbolizes the virility of Tammuz

58 Ornamental rein-ring from Ur. The wild ass is finely modelled in electrum. Rings of this sort (though without the ass) can be seen on the chariot-shafts in the bottom register of the Ur 'Standard' (*Ill. 46*)

characters of Gilgamesh and his companion Enkidu of the famous epic. This connexion has never in fact been proved and the hero remains anonymous, while the 'bull-man' can only vaguely be associated with the 'faun' figure of later mythology. Indeed, it would probably be idle to attempt the identification of all the images in these seals by reference to the scanty literary evidence available. For many of them are clearly mere devices, created 'on paper' to fill a space, and no more than figments of the seal-cutter's imagination.

The homogeneous linear design of these seals in the second phase is purely two-dimensional and the figures show little if any attempt at modelling. In the third phase (*Ill. 61*) a more sculptured treatment begins to appear and even the muscular system is carefully observed. There is little variation of the conventional themes, but towards the

→

Cylinder-seals from the first, second, and third Early Dynastic periods: 59 (*top*) 'Brocade' type, based on files of running animals. 60 (*middle*) Interlaced beasts and mythical figures create a frieze-pattern of unvarying density. 61 (*bottom*) Panels left blank for inscription articulate self-contained groups of figures, now more carefully modelled

62 Statue of a priest from Khafaje. The stylized formality of an earlier period has here given way to representational interest in detail

63 The largest pair of 'worshipper' statues from Tell Asmar. The male figure, on account of its height (thirty inches) and the symbols carved on its base, has been taken by some to represent the god Abu himself. Set in base of the female statue are the legs of a child

→

end of the period a new development is apparent. Empanelled inscriptions are introduced into the design and their appearance has the unexpected effect of improving its aesthetic quality. In their frieze-like repetition, the unbroken sequences of animated figures, engaged in violent activity, had obviously become wearisome to the eye, and they benefited greatly from division into self-contained groups. A new rhythm was created by the regular punctuation which the inscriptions provided. Mesopotamian seal-carving had now attained an unprecedented degree of artistic accomplishment. It reached a yet higher standard of perfection in Akkadian times, when the scope of the subject was dramatically widened, the seal-cutter appearing undaunted by the complexity of the religious scenes which he was expected to compress within so small a space.

Besides relief and carving there is Sumerian sculpture in the round. A great deal of this is today available for study, and it has for the most part been unearthed during the past thirty years. No specialized knowledge is needed to enable one to appreciate the curious appeal of these strange statues of rulers, priests, and ordinary worshippers. They were almost without exception made for and accordingly found among the ruins of Sumerian temples. Some of them come from excavations in the Diyala cities east of Baghdad; others from Ur in the extreme south of Iraq, or from Mari, a city on the Middle Euphrates, now lying within the Syrian frontier. But they all conform to the same recognizable stylistic conventions and to the same principles of formal abstraction.

The purpose of these statues is clear. An individual contrived for himself in stone a sculptured substitute to worship on his behalf. This is confirmed by the actual words used when such statues are inscribed. 'It offers prayers' is the unequivocal superscription of one from Lagash, and in another a specific intercession is prefaced by the formula—'Statue, say to my king (god) . . .' The statue speaks directly to the cult-image, just as the supplicant himself would speak to his god. Unfortunately no authentic example of such cult-image has as yet been found. At Tell Asmar on the Diyala, a collection of twenty-one discarded statues was discovered buried beneath the floor of a temple-sanctuary (*Ill. 63, 64*); and they included two abnormally tall figures with exaggeratedly large inlaid eyes. The male statue was also distinguished by the emblems of a vegetation cult sculptured on its base, while the figure of a child had been inset into that of the female. On this evidence, Frankfort identified the statues as cult-figures; but there is a strong argument for rejecting this conclusion. Like all the other statues in the group, they stand in the conventional attitude of worship and the hands clasped across their breasts hold small vessels for pouring libation. They also are worshippers, though probably a family of special distinction.

The Tell Asmar statues, together with a smaller group from Tell Agrab, represent the second phase of the Early Dynastic period. From the first, none have survived: so they alone show the earlier of two styles which succeeded one another in the development of purely Sumerian art. But before any finer distinctions of this sort are drawn, it may be well to consider the fundamental idiosyncrasies which set these early Mesopotamian sculptors apart from those of Egypt or for that matter of any other nationality in later times. One special disadvantage from which they suffered was the shortage of stone; nothing could more seriously hamper the work of a sculptor than this. In the plain of southern Iraq not a pebble is to be found, and for any purpose it must be imported from elswhere (*Ill. 66*). When one remembers the plentiful granite and limestone quarries of the Nile Valley, the contrast becomes obvious. An Egyptian king could afford to train an army of stonemasons without considering the wastage of stone. For the Sumerian sculptor's apprentice, on the other hand, practice-material was hard to come by and a spoilt trial-piece could be a serious matter. In spite of this, there is little evidence in early Sumerian carving of cautionary reticence. Necks are precariously slender; bent arms are freed from the stone and lower legs separated. The result may be gathered from the number of breakages to be seen, many of them mended by a clumsy system of dowelling. Later some attempt was made at least to remedy major weaknesses in the connexion between statue and base. 'Back-pillars'

65 Female head from Tell Agrab, Early Dynastic period. The hair was originally modelled in bitumen and protruded from beneath the head-cloth; the ears would have had ear-rings. The linen-fold head-dress lent itself to the characteristically formal style of earlier Sumerian sculpture

of stone were retained, or (as in the case of the Tell Asmar 'cult-statue') there was a disproportionate thickening of the ankles.

A term such as 'cautionary reticence' brings one now to the subject of sculptural style. We must next consider the formal principles of design, which these early artists seem to have devised (unconsciously, for they would have been no more capable of expressing them in words than the abstract interpretation of their own myths). Their central problem was to create a three-dimensional symbol, based on the shape of the human body but capable of asserting its own independent reality in space. It has been suggested that in Mesopotamia as in Egypt this was done by approximating the general shape of the statue to some simple geometrical form, and that, whereas the Egyptians preferred a cube, Sumerian sculptures were usually based on a cylinder or cone. This is an ingenious theory and has been argued in great detail. It provides, for instance, a reason why the seated statues, which are so familiar and satisfying a feature of Egyptian sculpture, when attempted in Sumer so often resulted in

66 Group of coloured stone mace-heads from Tell Agrab. Mace-heads were sometimes engraved with patterns or, as in most of those shown here, were polished to display the natural qualities of the stone. They illustrate the rarity-value of coloured stone in an alluvial country

conspicuous failure. Yet it seems an over-elaboration. If the abstractions of modern critical thought are momentarily stripped from one's mind, an obvious connexion presents itself between this regional disparity of styles and the varying forms in which the stone was available. In Egypt, the uncompromisingly prismatic blocks provided by the quarries (as well as the intimate association of sculpture with architecture), must be contrasted with the miscellaneous boulders imported by the Sumerians and the 'portable' character of the statues into which they were transformed.

But in any case, nothing can alter the fact that the process of formal simplification, applied equally by the Sumerians to general shapes and to details such as garments, hair (*Ill. 64*), and the naked human body, serves most effectively to express the significance of these statues and to invest them with an authentic originality which excites our admiration. Increasing sophistication might have been expected to result in a further geometrical simplification: but the case proved quite otherwise. A new stylistic development in the final

67 One of the rare examples of a seated Sumerian statue, from Mari on the Middle Euphrates, showing how characteristics of the later naturalistic style came to be standardized even in the remoter parts of Mesopotamia. The conspicuous use of a drill in carving the beard is an unusual feature of this figure

phase of the Early Dynastic period diverted the artist's interest from the austerities of sound carving to portraiture and the modelling of naturalistic detail (*Ill. 62*).

It is with pleasure as well as interest that one regards this strange galaxy of later Sumerian statuary (*Ill. 62–5, 67*). The places where it has been found are widely separated geographically, and the materials used are consequently varied. In many cases the richness of the stone itself is enhanced by the addition of pigment and inlay. The majority of female statues date from this period. Eyes and eyebrows are inlaid and the ears sometimes pierced for small gold ear-rings. The elaborate Sumerian coiffure is often modelled separately in bitumen. (As we have already mentioned, careful observation of its details suggests a reconstruction for the famous head-dresses from Ur differing very considerably from those which were tentatively made before these statues were discovered.) Statues in other material than stone, as we have seen in the 'Royal Cemetery' at Ur, were by no means beyond the capacity of the Sumerian craftsman. Naked human figures of bronze, standing on four ornamental legs (*Ill. 68*), seem to have been a common feature of the ritual furniture in shrines; and fragments of one such statue from Tell Agrab show it to have been more than half-life-size. From Tell Agrab also comes the exquisite

68 Copper statue from Khafaje. An offering-bowl would have been fixed to the head. The figure is naked except for a belt; he may be a mythological hero (compare cylinder-seals, *Ill. 60, 61*) or an ordinary human being. A new naturalism is now appearing in Sumerian art

69 Model chariot from Tell Agrab. The group is badly corroded; but the delicate modelling of the four asses' heads can still be appreciated. The chariot has solid wheels with studded rims; it has no body, and the charioteer stands on treads above the axle. This little group is the earliest known example of the *cire perdue* technique of casting bronze

model in bronze of a two-wheeled chariot drawn by four wild asses and driven by a bearded Sumerian (*Ill. 69*). The casting of this object is the earliest example known of the *cire perdue* process.

The transition from Sumerian to Akkadian rule in Mesopotamia seems to have been the outcome of peaceful penetration by a Semitic people and their gradual predominance among the ruling classes. One day perhaps we shall know more about Akkadian art, and it may confirm the impression we already have of technical competence and high aesthetic standards. But as yet, even Agade, the capital of Sargon, most illustrious of Akkadian kings, remains undiscovered and our knowledge depends on isolated works of art, such as the life-size bronze head of an Akkadian king, found in a sounding at Nineveh (*Ill. 70*) and the magnificent sculptured stela commemorating the victory of Naramsin over a mountain people (*Ill. 71*). If

70 Life-sized bronze head of an Akkadian king from Nineveh. The eyes, probably made of precious stones, have been removed. The elaborate treatment of the hair and beard contrasts with the smoothness of the face. This head, says Henri Frankfort, 'possesses a secular grandeur without precedent in Mesopotamia'

71 Stela of Naramsin. This marks a new understanding of
composition in relief; the diagonal emphasis is well adapted
to the shape of the stela. The upward surge of the victorious
army directs one's eye to the mountain-top. Naramsin
(wearing the horned crown of divinity) faces the dis-
ordered remnants of his foes; above him are the emblems
of his protecting gods

the first of these suggests to us a remarkable improvement in techno-
logical ability and material wealth, the second shows in its beautifully
modulated design, a freedom and confidence of expression far beyond
the ingenuous modesty of Eannatum's boundary-relief.

The rule of the Akkadian kings ended in disaster. Mesopotamia
was overrun by the Guti, barbaric mountain tribes from Iran, and
half a century of political chaos followed. Of all the Sumerian cities
only Lagash seems somehow to have remained aloof from these
disturbances and under its famous governor, Gudea, must have become an oasis of cultural tranquillity. Surviving works sculptured
in honour of this ruler bear witness to a sort of posthumous blossoming of Sumerian tradition (*Ill. 72–3*). As sculpture, indeed, they

72 Diorite statue of
Gudea, governor of La-
gash. The hard stone is
carved with complete mas-
tery and brought to a
perfect finish. The face is
still conventionalized, but
the muscles, for instance
of the right arm, are carefully studied

73 Another head of Gudea. He wears the turban-like head-dress that appears in most of his statues; the convention for representing the eyebrows should be noted. This series of heads well illustrates the combination of serenity and forcefulness achieved by the Lagash sculptors

74 Treasure from Alaca Hüyük. On the left and right are
a flagon and chalice of gold; in the centre, a copper disk
perhaps symbolizing the sun; beneath it, a gold brooch.
These objects come from a group of royal burials at present
confined to eastern Anatolia

perhaps excel anything previously accomplished. Their early discovery by French archaeologists towards the end of the last century,
established them for a whole generation as models by which
Sumerian art was judged.

ANATOLIA

As we approach the end of the third millennium B.C., we are
reaching a point where civilization can no longer have been confined
to the two great river valleys. To a greater or lesser extent it must
already have spread to the neighbouring countries of the Near East,
and here we should now expect to find evidence of independent
artistic development. In fact, it is surprising to discover how little
there is to merit our serious attention. In Iran, for instance, no

75 Stag-finial from a pole-top, Alaca Hüyük. It is made of copper, with the head plated in gold and electrum inlay. The style has affinities with that found in pre-Scythian nomadic art

evidence has survived of cultural development during this early period, and written history does not begin until the time of the Akkadian kings, who recorded their military campaigns against the State of Elam. Little more is known about Palestine or Syria in the third millennium, and it is not until we turn northwards towards Anatolia that we can catch a glimpse at least of good taste and fine craftsmanship during the Early Bronze Age.

There are two main sources of such material. One is the ruins of Troy, where Schliemann discovered 'treasures' of gold and silver, dating from a period a thousand years earlier than that with which he was concerned, and to which he understandably attributed them.

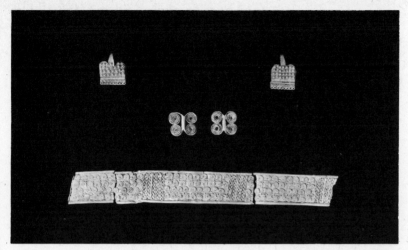

76 Some of the gold jewellery excavated by Schliemann at Troy. At the top, two pendant ear-rings; in the centre, double-spiral pins which show similarities with gold-work from Alaca Hüyük; at the bottom, a gold bracelet

The other source is the now famous cemetery at Alaca Hüyük, from which Turkish archaeologists (again seeking Hittite remains of a later period) recovered an astonishingly rich collection of metal objects. Both groups are now dated to the twenty-fourth or twenty-fifth centuries B.C.; and they suggest that three hundred years or so after the Sumerians had made their unconscious bequest to posterity in the 'Royal Cemetery' at Ur, comparable craftsmanship had begun to appear in the remote uplands of the Anatolian plateau.

The cemetery at Alaca Hüyük, like that at Ur, was not indisputably 'Royal', though in this case there was no reason for suspecting any kind of ritual immolation. Male or female dead (occasionally both together) were buried in rather large shaft-graves, roofed over with logs of wood and surrounded by certain ritual-objects, as well as by their personal possessions (men by their weapons and women by ornaments and toilet requisites). Ritual contrivances most characteristic of these treasures are the so-called 'standards'—metal figures of bulls or stags, with their feet drawn together to fit on to the head of a pole—and strange metal grilles, also sometimes ornamented with animal figures, which for want of a better name have been described as 'sun-disks'. Ornamental heads for the poles supporting a canopy or catafalque would probably best suggest their purpose, as the poles had golden handles which also survived. These and many other curious objects—personal ornaments, utensils, weapons, and the curious metal figurines of a primitive cult— variously suggest proficiency in technical processes, such as smelting, hammering, soldering, *repoussé* work, and the *cire perdue* process of casting (*Ill. 74–7*).

When first discovered, though its elegance was dimly reflected in the 'treasures' from Troy on the remote Aegean coast, this Alaca tomb-furniture seemed such an isolated manifestation of 'high life' in an otherwise rather pedestrian archaeological landscape, that it has sometimes been taken to indicate the temporary rule of a foreign aristocracy. But more recently indications have been found at other Anatolian sites that similar cemeteries existed (one of them unfortunately rendered inaccessible by a modern graveyard); and future excavations may well bring the Early Bronze cultures of Anatolia into higher artistic repute.

77 Jewellery from the royal tombs of Alaca Hüyük. Beads and gold pins. The craftsmanship here is of a remarkably high standard

PART FOUR

Development and Diffusion
in the Second Millennium B.C.

MIDDLE KINGDOM ART IN EGYPT

While Mesopotamia was being overrun and its regional dynasties disorganized by barbarian tribes from Iran, Egypt was slowly recovering from the effects of equally serious political upheavals. The central authority of the Pharaohs had been challenged and temporarily overthrown by a feudal nobility, who, during the century and a half known as the First Intermediate period, brought civil war and anarchy to the whole country. Political stability and the unity of the State were eventually restored during the last fifty years of the third millennium by a Pharaoh of the Eleventh Dynasty, Menthu-hetep II, and during the so-called Middle Kingdom which followed there was a slow revival of Egyptian artistic traditions.

Yet much had changed. Psychologically the Egyptian people could hardly have remained unaffected by the wholesale disruption of their social life and economy over so long a period. In fact, their complacent belief in the immutable stability of their private world had been badly shaken. This is directly reflected in the art of their time. There is a new metaphysical approach to the nature and meaning of temporal authority; a new emphasis on the gravity of a ruler's responsibility as opposed to the majestic infallibility with which royalty invests him. Many writers on the subject have commented on this changed aspect of Middle Kingdom portraiture, and have seen in the brooding and melancholy expressions of the Eleventh and Twelfth Dynasty Pharaohs something comparable to the predominant pessimism of the written precepts which they passed on to their successors (*Ill. 78–9*). Aldred, for instance, notices how the royal statues of the age '. . . have little of the god-like geniality or even the regality of the Old Kingdom Pharaonic sculptures. The heads that wear the Middle Kingdom crowns lie uneasy; and instead, the expression is almost brutal or severe: at the

78 Head of King Amenemhet III in basalt. The hardness of the material gives it an archaic appearance, but this may be in part a deliberate antiquarian return to some of the traditions of the Old Kingdom

most sympathetic, it is sad and introspective.' From the aesthetic viewpoint he sees that '. . . so far from disengaging itself further from its stone matrix, the sculptured form seeks to shrink into it, as though for sanctuary. The deceased is no longer shown striding forward, alert, eager, in all the pride of a healthy physique. Instead, lacking such assurance he has retired into a bleaker contemplation, pulling his cloak around him.'

But there were other circumstances which had contributed to a change in the character of Middle Kingdom sculpture. Among them was a new development in religious belief. During the early centuries

79 Head of Senusret III in red quartzite. The refinement of this head and the delicate modelling of the flesh, gives it an expressiveness unusual in Egyptian sculpture. Critics have spoken of its 'pensive melancholy' and 'haunting humanity'

of the monarchy, the worship of the sun-god, Ra—a religion sponsored by the learning and authority of the theological college at Heliopolis—had gained a monopoly of nation-wide prestige and had eventually been adopted by the Pharaohs of the Fifth and Sixth Dynasties as a royal cult. But in more recent times a rival faith, connected with the worship of Osiris, had begun to gain ground as a popular interpretation of human destiny. One can see in Osiris, as in Tammuz of Mesopotamia, the mythological figure of a 'dying-god', evoked by the fertility worship of a remoter age. By the beginning of the Eleventh Dynasty, however, his cult had become firmly established in its own holy city at Abydos in Upper Egypt, where he now presided as a god of the dead—a divinity who had himself suffered death and resurrection in the process of transfiguration. Since the religion of Ra had by then begun to deteriorate into a mere tradition of magic, this alternative creed, with its promise of abstract immortality, as opposed to mere survival within the confines of the tomb, seems to have provided some relief from the prevailing mood of disillusion.

All this materially affected the form of Middle Kingdom sculpture. The portrait-statue for instance lost much of its magical significance in the light of the new beliefs, and was either discarded altogether or considerably reduced in size (*Ill. 80*), while a new type of figure— the *ex voto* or temple-statue—showed a notable increase in popularity (e.g. *Ill. 82–3*). As in Mesopotamia, where its function was

81 Head of the Lady Sennuy, from a complete seated statue
in granite. Although discovered in Kerma, Sudan, a place
remote from the cultural centres, it is probably by one of
the court sculptors. It combines a restrained sense of form
with excellent workmanship and high finish, and in spite of
the rigid conventions, the peculiar charm of the subject is
perfectly conveyed

universally accepted, so in Egypt it now afforded to an absent worshipper the satisfaction of participation 'by proxy' in temple ceremonies. In the tombs meanwhile, even the coffins themselves had undergone a significant change in shape (*Ill. 86*). Instead of the traditional severity of the sarcophagus (for whose rectangularity we have elsewhere suggested a special significance), new and more elaborate shapes began to appear, approximating to the mummified image of Osiris himself. This rather macabre silhouette of a body swathed in sepulchral bandages becomes increasingly familiar from now on, symbolizing a concept which we ourselves can only half

83 Statue of Ameny. Like the previous example, this is an *ex voto* statue, of a type that was popular throughout the period. Ameny squats tailor-fashion in a long kilt which is stretched tight across his legs

understand, namely the ceremonial confinement of man's physical remains as a prerequisite of spiritual release. It is to be seen in the so-called 'Osiride' statues, associated with the funerary temples of the Middle Kingdom Pharaohs (*Ill. 87*). Like the 'block' statue, which was now adopted as a suitable form of *ex voto* (*Ill. 82–3*), these figures with their severely rectangular back-pillars well illustrate the 'engaged' character of contemporary design.

It would have been interesting to study the effects of new religious beliefs on funerary reliefs in royal tombs of the period, but unfortunately very little relevant material has survived. Our knowledge in

84 Copy of paintings from the tomb of Knum-Hetep, showing Asiatics bringing tribute to the dead man. This series of wall-paintings is on the whole rather dull. The figures are arranged in horizontal registers and the gestures are frozen and lifeless. The clearly painted details, however, give it great historical interest

→

85 Head of a woman with separate wig. Wood. The wig is painted black, and was decorated to simulate the gold tubes which women of high rank wore in their hair at this period. The inlaid eyes are missing, but the subtle modelling still gives the head a special distinction

86 Coffin of Steward Knum-Hetep, showing the gilded portrait-mask of the deceased wearing a heavy wig, bead 'hawk' collar, and the beard of Osiris, whose idealized form was usually given to the dead man. Carved and painted wooden coffins were now replacing stone sarcophagi

fact both of reliefs and of wall-paintings belonging to the Middle Kingdom is largely derived from the rock-cut tombs of noblemen overlooking such centres of feudal power as Meir, Beni Hasan, El Bersheh, and Thebes (*Ill. 90*). On the walls of these one observes incidentally that tempera-painting, which had hitherto been considered a poor substitute for painted reliefs, had now come into its own as an independent art worthy of the highest patronage (e.g. *Ill. 84*). There are new subjects in evidence, including battle scenes to remind one how recently the peace of the country had been disturbed by civil war and even by foreign invasion. There are hunting scenes from the tombs in Meir (*Ill. 90*) which may well have inspired Assyrian artists of later times; and from the same

88 Senusret I and the god Ptah. This is part of a pillar from Senusret's jubilee temple and shows the King in proud and confident companionship with the god. It is to be noticed that they have identical profiles. The relief-style is bold, with deep cutting and an emphasis on line, but with little modelling of the surface

⁷ Funerary statue of King ⁻nusret I. The King, swathed bandages, is shown in the ⁻ise of the mummified ⁻siris, god of the underworld. his hands he carried two kh, symbols of the resur-ction (damaged)

89 Model of a fishing-boat from the tomb of Meket-re. When a rich Egyptian died, replicas of everything that he might need in the after-life were placed in the tomb with him. Life-like models of servants, workshops, animals, stables, and boats complete with crews have all been found, and give us a vivid idea of the ordinary life of the time

90 Two reliefs from Meir, fine examples of incised drawing. *Left:* Ukhotep hunting; the King, as usual, is shown larger than his servant. *Right:* Herdsman with cattle. The herdsman is emaciated and old, but is portrayed with cynical humour rather than with compassion

source, there are some scenes, for instance that of a landowner watching the activities of his servants, where a new dynamic effect has been attained by the wide spacing of the figures and the novel device of depicting energetic action in serial movements. Another development is the multiplication in tombs of 'servant' figures in the round, which at times seem to fulfil much the same purpose as their counterparts in the reliefs and paintings (*Ill. 89*). Scores of neatly painted toy figures are grouped according to their various occupations in workshop and farm settings or manipulating boats.

Middle Kingdom art may have lacked in some degree the fresh inventiveness of earlier centuries; but there is much to admire in the little that has survived, and in the sculpture at least one sees the introspective disposition which prevailed at the time most ably expressed.

91 Hippopotamus. Blue faience. In this little figure it is easy to see the Egyptian's humorous regard for the ungainly beast, whose grossness is further emphasized by the delicate plants, birds, and butterflies that bedeck his flanks

The Middle Kingdom in Egypt and the Second Intermediate period which followed occupied the first half of the second millennium B.C.; this same period in Mesopotamia is artistically perhaps the least rewarding field of study in that country's early history. Indeed this is true of the greater part of the second millennium. Historically the period starts with the aftermath of Sumerian culture, surviving from the prosperous Third Dynasty of Ur into the succeeding epoch, when the hegemony of the southern city-states was shared between the rulers of Isin and Larsa. In the eighteenth century the whole land was once more united under Hammurabi, the first great king of Babylon, a city which now appears in history for the first time. And here again a curious freak of archaeological fortune is brought to mind. For in a dozen years of almost continuous excavation before the First World War, the German diggers at Babylon brought to light no single major work by which the art of its First Dynasty could be judged. Apart from cylinder-seals, a great quantity of small terracottas, and the relief at the head of the famous stela in the Louvre, bearing the text of Hammurabi's law-code (*Ill. 92*), we know nothing of early Babylonian art. Even the single King's head in the Louvre usually placed in this category, is indistinguishable in style from the work of Isin-Larsa or Ur III (*Ill. 93*).

Nor have the last-named periods bequeathed more than isolated fragments of sculpture. And this is strange; for architecturally at least they represent an epoch of great creative activity and many buildings of distinction dating from it have come to light. It was the time which saw first great *ziggurats* or 'staged towers', rising above their walled temple-enclosures, not only at Ur itself but at other great cities such as Eridu, Kish, Uruk, and Nippur; it was the time, too, of the great vaulted tombs at Ur and the royal palaces at Eshnunna, Ischali, and elsewhere. There is at least one seated statue from Ur (*Ill. 94*), and minor art-objects such as the fragment of a stone bowl with beautifully carved couchant ibexes from Ischali (*Ill. 95*). But the best-preserved statuary is from remote Mari on the Middle Euphrates, where an independent dynasty succumbed to the far-reaching ambition of Hammurabi (*Ill. 97-8*). Their palace has also provided us with the only considerable fragments of contemporary wall-painting (*Ill. 96*).

The sculpture then seems to suggest a prolongation of the Akkadian and Lagash traditions in an increasingly stereotyped form. Careful modelling of naked limbs is contrasted with an almost tedious formal treatment of the clothing, whose flounces and fringes lend themselves to elementary pattern. The result is a stylistic flavour which has come in time, quite erroneously, to be thought of as characteristically 'Babylonian'. As for the terracottas, the life-size monumental lions from the entrance to a Larsa period temple at Harmal, near Baghdad, show on what a large scale this material could be effectively handled (*Ill. 99*). The smaller objects are for the most part *ex voto* plaques, made repetitively in an open mould and probably sold in the vicinity of a temple (*Ill. 100–101*). Sometimes their subjects are mythological; at others they express the most elementary

92 Stela of Hammurabi. At the head of the stela inscribed with his law-code, Hammurabi stands confronting the sun-god, 'Lord of justice and law-giver.' The scene is portrayed in heavy rounded relief and neither the robes nor beards show any of the detailed modelling in which earlier periods had delighted

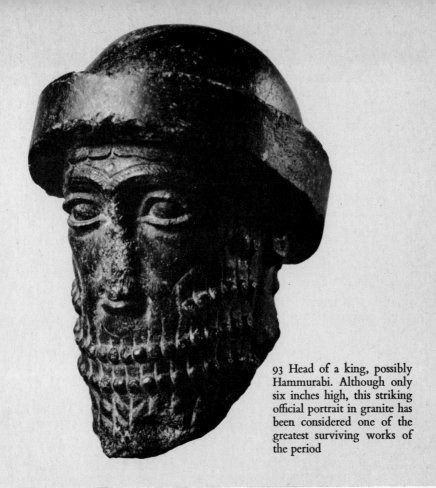

93 Head of a king, possibly Hammurabi. Although only six inches high, this striking official portrait in granite has been considered one of the greatest surviving works of the period

form of wish-fulfilment with a crudity which is occasionally amusing. The seals of the period are also artistically uninspired (*Ill. 102*). All the freedom of design and variety of subject which animated the carving of Akkadian times has vanished. There is now a standard scene in which a human figure is introduced by a mythical intermediary into the presence of a god. The individual figures are stereotyped in shape and monotonously erect.

The latter half of the second millennium was a period of transition in Mesopotamia. From the sixteenth century on, the southern cities were ruled by a foreign dynasty of uncertain Iranian lineage, known as the Kassites. But the Kassite domain was confined in the south by

94 Statuette of the goddess Ningal from Ur. Lacking any distinctive treatment of insignia, this statue would have been hard to date or identify without the inscription, which shows it to be a little earlier than Hammurabi

a 'Sea-land' Kingdom at the head of the Persian Gulf and in the north by an Indo-European people called Mitanni, who occupied the fertile country watered by the Middle Tigris and its tributaries, extending as far south as modern Kirkuk. From a cultural point of view, the Kassites made almost no impression on the Mesopotamian cities, since their modest origin left them no alternative to accepting the long-established pattern of Babylonian civilization complete as they found it. Temples and palaces continued to be extended or rebuilt in the style of the century. At Dur Kurigalzu ('Aqarquf), where the well-preserved core of the vast *ziggurat* still makes a conspicuous landmark in the plain, painted frescoes are used to ornament the base of the walls in the royal palace—a precedent which anticipated the sculptured reliefs of Assyrian palaces in later times.

95 Green stone bowl from Ischali, with ibex in relief. There would have been two more ibexes repeated on the missing sides of the bowl. The heads are modelled in the round while the bodies are in relief. The natural form is beautifully adapted to the shape of the object

Elsewhere moulded bricks were now also used for ornament (*Ill. 104*), as they afterwards continued to be for a thousand years. At 'Aqarquf too, isolated fragments of sculpture were found—a painted limestone head (*Ill. 103*) which by its resemblance to contemporary work of the Amarnah period in Egypt reminded one of the close connexion between the two countries at this time (the text has survived of an entertaining correspondence between Amenophis III and a Kassite king containing mutual criticism of presents exchanged on the occasion of a royal marriage), and sensitive terracotta figures of animals (*Ill. 105*).

The excavation of a Mitannian city at Nuzi, near Kirkuk, produced much interesting inscribed material. Nevertheless, very little is known of Mitannian art, save for a particularly fine painted pottery

96 Fragment of wall-painting from Mari. This is one of the earliest wall-paintings in Mesopotamia. Figures wearing fringed shawls and the felt cap of North Syria with ceremonial ornaments. The decorative scheme is interesting, using trees, human figures, and mythological motifs indiscriminately for visual effect

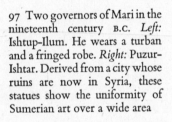

97 Two governors of Mari in the nineteenth century B.C. *Left:* Ishtup-Ilum. He wears a turban and a fringed robe. *Right:* Puzur-Ishtar. Derived from a city whose ruins are now in Syria, these statues show the uniformity of Sumerian art over a wide area

with designs in white paint on a dark ground (*Ill. 107*), and cylinder-seals which set the standard for North Syrian carving for several centuries (*Ill. 108–10*). But it is in turning northward once more to Anatolia that we find the most conspicuously individual art-developments of the period.

The civilization of Mesopotamia was first brought to Anatolia early in the second millennium by colonies of Assyrian merchants who settled in Cappadocia and elsewhere to establish trading-stations. One of these at Kültepe near Kayseri has been excavated; and, in the process of recovering tens of thousands of clay tablets

98 Offering-bearer from Mari. He carries in his arms a victim for sacrifice. The rendering of the beard and the tasselled cloak point to a date in the nineteenth century B.C.

which constituted the business archives of the colony, much was also learnt about the indigenous Middle Bronze Age peoples of the Anatolian plateau. But it was also possible among the personal names mentioned in the tablets to detect traces of an intrusive Indo-European element in the population, later to be identified as the Hittites, who subsequently united the cities of eastern Anatolia into a single State. An aptitude for political and military organization enabled these people to extend their dominion southwards beyond the Taurus into Cilicia and North Syria, where they came into conflict with the Egyptians. The peak of their prosperity was in the fourteenth and thirteenth centuries B.C., when their kings ruled over a considerable empire with its capital at Hattusas (Boghazköy) in the bend of the Halys River.

Representative examples of Hittite sculpture, dating from the 'Imperial' epoch, have survived both in the form of guardian figures from the city-gates at Boghazköy and of rock-sculptures in religious shrines. In both cases their archaeological setting does much to invest them with a romantic interest which easily impresses itself on one's memory. But, removed from this special context and judged by the more rigid standards of aesthetic criticism, they show little evidence of any genuine capacity for creative expression, or for that matter of technical ability. Probably the most striking are

102 Cylinder-seal from the time of Hammurabi. These seals
contain an amazing wealth of fine-detailed engraving. Here the
seal-owner is being presented to the gods Shamash and Ishtar
by a mythological intermediary. Typically Mesopotamian
elements are the opposed goats and the cow and suckling calf

the famous reliefs in the rock-sanctuary at Yazilikaya, near Boghazköy (*Ill. 113–14*). But here as elsewhere it is not easy to dissociate
the intrinsic merit of their design from the dramatic effects of the
setting chosen for them—mysterious clefts in the rock which could
only be approached through a series of man-made antechambers.
The pageant of deities in their outer sanctuary proves to have been
inspired by a foreign queen who seems to have been less interested
in portraying the Hittite gods than those of a neighbouring State
called Kizzuwatna. Nevertheless, the whole atmosphere of the shrine
evokes the mythological climate of ancient Hattusas and emphasizes
the preoccupation of its inhabitants with the symbolic security of
the rocks among which it was built. The relief-figure in the inner
sanctuary of the young King embraced by a god, carries a force of
conviction which can only be the outcome of strongly felt religious
emotion, while the great dagger, buried in the rock before him,
creates a sculptural device no less arresting in its symbolism (*Ill. 114*).

103 Limestone head of the Kassite period from Dur Kurigalzu. Originally painted in black and red, the style is reminiscent of contemporary carving in Egypt. The moustache is kept short, and the beard full

Of the Boghazköy portal-sculptures the figure in relief from the so-called 'Warrior Gate' is the best known, as well as being the best preserved. Archaeologically its subject is of great interest (it was at one time thought to represent an Amazon) and its style has been considered, perhaps rightly, as characteristically Hittite. But as a work of art, if judged for instance by the criteria of the contemporary Eighteenth Dynasty in Egypt, it is quite unremarkable. As for the animal and hybrid figures, those in the 'Sphinx Gate' have at least some interest as initiating a sculptural device later much

141

104 Façade ornament from a Kassite temple at Warka. Male and female deities bear the 'flowing vase' from which streams of water, perhaps symbolical of the 'twin rivers', fall to the ground on either side. The ornament is an integral part of the architecture, the façade being built up of moulded bricks

105 Terracotta head of a lioness. Another example of
sensitive modelling in clay in Kassite times (cf.
Ill. 99). Like the head in *Ill. 103* this comes from
Dur Kurigalzu

popularized in Assyria, namely the 'twin-aspect' portal-figure with
five legs. But taken as a whole the quality of this sculpture does not
compare favourably with that of the architecture at Boghazköy, all
of which seems to have been massively conceived and impressively
accomplished.

The Hittite kings, in their campaigns of conquest south of Taurus,
found themselves in conflict with the armies of Egypt protecting
her Syrian dependencies. Syria and Palestine had in fact now become
'debatable lands', dominated alternatively by the greater Powers of
the Near East. Throughout the second millennium there was hardly
a time when they were not wholly or in part subjected to the rule of
Egyptian, Mesopotamian, or Hittite kings. At intervals some small

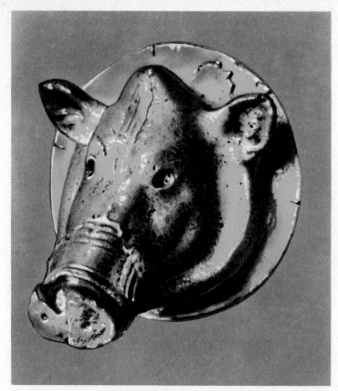

106 Boar's head in faience, from Nuzi. Such bosses were widely used as wall-ornaments in Mesopotamian buildings

107 Mitannian painted pottery from Atchana (Alalakh). The pots are ornamented in white on a dark ground, with formalized patterns usually derived from nature. Such 'Nuzi ware' is found throughout Assyria and North Syria from the fifteenth to thirteenth centuries B.C.

Principality would assert its independence, only to be swamped in the outbreak of some new imperial conflict. In this world of unremitting political upheaval, no sort of cultural continuity could be maintained nor could regional art be expected to develop along individual lines: and this circumstance may explain why the countries of the Levant, which were distinguished as the birth-place of two world religions and much fine literature, lack any notable artistic tradition in ancient times.

It is indeed evident that political centres such as Byblos, Ras Shamra (*Ill. 117*), and Megiddo (*Ill. 112*), did in the rare intervals of tranquillity endeavour to emulate the grandeur of Babylon or Thebes; we possess remarkable samples of their jewellery, metal-

Three examples of Mitannian cylinder-seals: 108 (*top left*)
The winged disk represents the sky, supported by a pillar,
reflecting Mitannian ideas on cosmology. Note the garments with their heavy folds. 109 (*bottom left*) Bull-man
and goddess destroying a lion, and a 'sacred tree'. 110
(*above*) Seated figure drinking through a metal tube, with
attendant and other space-filling motifs

work, and even sculpture. But the workmanship of such examples
as are not actually imported from Egypt or elsewhere, is so notably
inferior and the derivative character of the designs so tedious that
they lack other than archaeological interest. Rare exceptions exist,
particularly among Sir Leonard Woolley's finds from ancient
Atchana, of which *Ill. 115* is a good example. This small city on the
Orontes became politically conspicuous under a king called Yarimlim
in the eighteenth century B.C., and thereafter enjoyed intermittent
periods of prosperity. The sculptured head here illustrated, which is
thought to be a portrait of Yarimlim, is perhaps the only piece of
statuary found in Syria which is demonstrably the work of a
thoroughly competent artist.

111 Painted clay dog, found in the Assyrian trading-station (*karum*) of Kültepe. It is an example of the fanciful polychrome pottery produced and traded at this time

112 Winged griffin in ivory from Megiddo: a masterpiece of this school of ivory-workers, so impressive that it is hard to realize that it is only one and a half inches high. Compare the stylization of this ivory with the freedom later achieved in the same medium (*Ill. 173–6*)

Hittite carvings at Yazili-kaya: 113 (*above*) Line of running warriors. Each wears a high ribbed cap, a garment with a short skirt held by a belt at the waist, and shoes with upturned toes. 114 (*right*) A young king is embraced by his protecting god. On the left is a huge sculptured dagger with symbolically ornamented hilt, which appears to be stuck point-downwards in the rock

115 Head of Yarimlin of Alalakh. This is one of the few pieces of sculpture found in Syria that are obviously the work of genuine artists

116 Ivory lid of a box from Minet-el-Beida. A goddess, the 'Queen of the wild beasts', is seated and wears a necklace and a diadem round her hair. Goats thrust up their heads, as though reaching for the vegetation that she holds

117 Gold bowl from Ras Shamra. A remarkable synthesis of Egyptian and Mesopotamian motifs. In the inner circle are wild goats. The outer circle shows bulls and gazelles hunted from a chariot; dogs are also in the field

PART FIVE

New Kingdom Sophistication in Egypt

After the half-truths and makeshift of so much provincial art, one returns with relief to the metropolitan work of New Kingdom artists in Egypt. Many epithets have been used to describe the quality which distinguishes the sculpture and painting of the Eighteenth Dynasty from all that preceded it, and among them 'exhibitionist' seems one of the least complimentary. But in its original meaning this word implies no more than a suggestion of 'show' or exuberant display, and, at the height of their imperial greatness, the Egyptians were well entitled to a little of either, provided it did not alter or impair their aesthetic tradition. And of this there could in fact be little danger, since their innate conservatism alone sufficed to protect the primary forms of their culture from the effects of ephemeral taste or fashionable experiment. But the trend of fashion throughout the period and the character of the experiments are themselves of interest, and to understand them we must look at the political events on which they so closely depended.

The invasion of Egypt by the Hyksos 'Shepherd Kings' in the seventeenth century B.C. was part of the same far-reaching migratory movement of peoples which brought Indo-European Hittites into Anatolia and Greeks into the Aegean. Their occupation of the Delta caused a second major break of the thread of Egyptian Dynastic history; but it left a legacy of material advantage, the effects of which soon became evident. New methods of warfare, including the use of horse-drawn chariots, which had made their onslaught irresistible, were now adopted by the Pharaonic armies and opened for them in their turn a period of foreign conquest. No more than a century after the final expulsion of the Hyksos, Egypt had regained her position as a premier world Power with an empire extending from the Sudan to the Euphrates.

The history of the Eighteenth Dynasty falls into four distinct phases, during each of which political changes are reflected in new artistic developments. First there is a period of military successes and imperial expansion, during which able and energetic kings enriched their country with the spoils of foreign conquest. It also covers an interval of about thirty years when, as in Elizabethan England, the scene at home was dominated by the striking figure of a powerful queen, the woman-Pharaoh Hatshepsut. She personified the newly conceived imperial destiny of her people and gave new inspiration to the artists and writers of her court. Next there are three reigns during which long intervals of peace and security gave respite from political cares and leisure to enjoy the fruits of conquest. Expanding commerce and foreign trade could by then provide material luxuries unheard of in earlier times and increasing familiarity with foreign ideas resulted in new forms of cultural enrichment. Indeed, a point had been reached where a surfeit of such amenities might well have resulted in weaknesses such as egoism and self-indulgence, had not such tendencies been curbed by a newly found habit of self-discipline. The years of imperial expansion had made heavy demands on the moral resources of the Egyptian people and a new ideal of public service had taken shape. The individualism of an earlier feudal society had in fact given place to a corporate sense of obligation to the interests of the State.

All this is reflected in the earlier art of the Eighteenth Dynasty, which has been considered the height of classical Egyptian expression. It is to be seen in particular at Thebes, which had now become the capital of the Empire and the seat of a new State-religion, the worship of its city-god Amen having replaced the cult of Heliopolitan Ra.

In the third phase there is a complete change of scene corresponding to the so-called 'Amarnah Revolution'—a social and spiritual upheaval brought about by the eccentricities of a single remarkable individual, the apostate Pharaoh Amenhetep IV, later known as Akhenaten. The cult of Amen was now temporarily discarded in favour of a new monotheistic faith, symbolized by worship of the sun-disk, Aten, and a complicated 'quietist' philosophy. The capital

118 Banquet scene from the tomb of the butler Wah. The girl musicians dance as they play. A serving-maid offers a guest wine. The draughtsmanship is sure, but prosaic, and the interest of line predominates over that of colour

was moved to a new site, today known as Tell-el-Amarnah: and there for some years the King devoted himself to metaphysical speculation, while the disintegration of his neglected Empire passed almost unnoticed. His death was followed by an aftermath of reaction, which constitutes the fourth and final phase of the period. The Amarnah city and the cult of Aten were simultaneously abandoned and the ascendancy of Thebes restored. After an interval of political and artistic compromise under the young king, Tut-ankh-amon, the fortunes of the Empire and the classical orientation of Egyptian art were finally and effectively restored through the timely intervention of an unpretentious realist, Horemheb.

With this remarkable cycle of political events as a background, it is hardly surprising to find in the panorama of Eighteenth Dynasty art repeated and unmistakable symptoms of spiritual conflict.

153

119 Queen Hatshepsut's mother, as depicted in a relief from Hatshepsut's mortuary temple at Deir-el-Bahri. The Middle Kingdom influence is still strong enough to keep the 'official' style of relief-sculpture almost unchanged

Beneath a misleading appearance of superficial uniformity, it is in fact compounded of manifold paradoxes; and it is easy to enumerate conflicting factors in the predicament which they caused. Enjoyment of current prosperity was restrained by memories of recent political disasters, just as pride in national unity was tempered by the prospect of foreign rivalry and conflict. Among individuals, increasing opportunity for initiative was frustrated by traditional conservatism

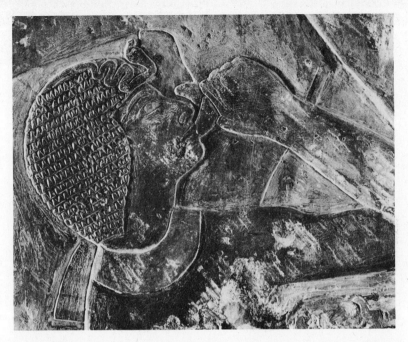

120 Detail from the mortuary chapel of Queen Hatshepsut, showing the Queen drinking from the udder of Hathor. Hathor was worshipped as the protectress of the city of the dead. In the Queen's hair the protecting pharaonic snake (uraeus) can be seen. Traces of colour remain

and the impulse to personal piety hampered by the authoritarian dogma of State-religion. 'Despite the military and aggressive character of the age, the ideal was a feminine one.'

There is specific evidence of this situation in the surviving works of the period (*Ill. 118–23*). Perhaps the most varied and abundant material for study is to be found among the reliefs and paintings in the early New Kingdom tombs, mostly concentrated in the vast necropolis at Thebes and covering more than two centuries of Egyptian history. Rock-cut chambers had now been adopted as burying-places for royalty and commoners alike. For reasons of security, kings were buried without ostentation and their mortuary

121 Hunting scene from the tomb of Menna. Menna is seen in duplicate, hunting wildfowl with a boomerang and spearing fish. He is accompanied by his family, including a small naked daughter who has become interested in the water-plants. It is hard to see in this picture more than the anticipated nostalgia of the dead for the pleasures of life, which at this time can scarcely have been negligible

buildings located some miles away in the West Theban plain, where a long process of architectural elaboration now converted them into magnificent temples, which could be dedicated jointly to the memory of the ruler and the glory of the god Amen. Outstanding among such buildings is the huge mortuary temple at Deir-el-Bahri, erected by the architect Sen-Mut for Queen Hatshepsut. With its astonishingly beautiful arrangement of three rising colonnaded terraces, perfectly exploiting the dramatic possibilities of the site on which it is built, this remains one of the most imposing temples of ancient Egypt. Within its colonnades, the walls are decorated with low relief illustrating both religious subjects and episodes in the Queen's reign, and these are all the more important because little other mortuary sculpture of the Eighteenth Dynasty has survived (*Ill. 120*).

Cut into the soft limestone of the West Theban hills are also the tomb-chapels of court officials. They are for the most part decorated with gouache-painting on a wall-coating of plaster, and they recall the Middle Kingdom tradition which established wall-painting as an independent art. The scenes depicted here are very varied indeed, but almost without exception concern themselves with some aspect or other of the owner's life on earth (*Ill. 122–3*). One notices that in particular the pleasurable aspects of life seem to be emphasized, as indeed might be expected in an age of luxury and conspicuous elegance. The homely Old Kingdom scene—that of the owner receiving gifts at his offering-table, for instance—has now become a banquet with garlanded guests, music, and perfumed dancers, over which he and his family preside with manifestly sensuous enjoyment, in strange contrast to the dedicated austerity of funerary scenes in

122 Paintings from the unlocated tomb of Neb-Amon. The vigorous drawing of the horses should be noted; the chariots are very similar to those which were actually found in the tomb of Tut-ankh-amon

earlier times. But in addition to such scenes of feasting, and other relaxations such as fishing or fowling expeditions in the marshes, the owner is also often seen taking his official position in political or military functions—training recruits or receiving distinguished foreigners. One's first impression, therefore, is that these pictures are aimed at the simple purpose of creating a biographical memorial of his life. But in the end one wonders whether their true purpose may not go beyond mere monumentality, or the elementary magic of wish-fulfilment, to some more esoteric function; an assertion or testimony of belief in some metaphysical principle. 'These scenes are

quite literally concerned with eternal values; namely, the immanent values of life such as power, wealth, and abundance, seen *sub specie aeternitatis*.' This interpretation by Mrs Frankfort may well be less extravagantly imaginative than it at first sounds.

Where tomb-statues are concerned, on the other hand, there is no longer any reason to doubt the simplicity of their purpose. During the impoverished days of the Hyksos invasion, they had steadily become smaller until they could actually be enclosed in the human-shaped coffins of the period, and were soon hardly distinguishable from the *shabti* figures which had largely replaced the little toy

123 Scenes of feasting also from the tomb of Neb-Amon. In the top row sit guests wearing perfume-cones on their heads. The bottom register shows musicians (two of them drawn full-face, a practice hitherto unheard of) and dancers, whose gestures are those of modern Arab dancing. The musicians show the soles of their feet

124 Three views of a little Negro girl carrying a jar. It is made of boxwood and is four inches tall. Such a degree of naturalism is outside the main tradition of Egyptian art, but was permitted in the portrayal of menials (cf. *Ill. 123*) when it would have been forbidden in 'official' art. The artist has returned with obvious relish to the observation of anatomy and the expression of graceful exertion

servants of the Middle Kingdom. Now, in the prosperous days of the early Eighteenth Dynasty, they reappear as a prominent feature of the shrine. Their original magico-religious function has been forgotten and they have become merely official memorials of the deceased. Other forms of statuary include an increasing number of *ex voto* figures, erected in the temple-precincts by individuals specially privileged to do so. Servant figures also do occasionally reappear, but their place is no longer in the tomb. In a profane world of

growing sophistication they have acquired a novel function as supports for toilet vessels (*Ill. 124*).

During the early part of the dynasty it was the great metropolis of Thebes which provided a centre of gravity for the cultural and religious life of the nation. The task of expelling the Hyksos from Lower Egypt had fallen to the Theban princes, and they were now able to watch the gradual recovery of the Delta from the devastation which the invasion had caused. Culturally, the northern cities were bound to be affected by a century of alien occupation, and in the realm of art foreign influences now began to be unmistakably apparent. Foreign goldsmiths from Crete are already thought to have established their workshops in Memphis, and to their presence are attributed idiosyncrasies of style which now appear for the first

164

125 (*above*) Cretan tribute-bearers from the tomb of Sen-Mut. Not only are Minoan garments and vessels accurately depicted, but the Egyptian artist has here deliberately attempted a stylistic pastiche of Cretan wall-painting. 126 (*left*) A garden-pool. The scene is viewed from several different angles, so that everything can be appreciated at its best: the pool from above, the fishes and ducks in profile, and so on. The flowers include red poppies and papyrus plants

time in Egyptian jewellery, giving to its design a distinctively Aegean character. Amongst these are draughtsmen's devices such as the so-called 'flying gallop' and 'cavalier perspective', a term which merely implies the appearance of a scene to someone mounted on horseback. In the tomb of Queen Hatshepsut's architect, Sen-Mut at Thebes, there is even a scene of Cretan tribute-bearers in which, in addition to correctly depicting Minoan costume, the artist has adopted his actual style to the alien formulas of Cretan art (*Ill. 125*).

It is easy to imagine that the peculiarly light-hearted elegance of the Minoan world ('*homo ludens*'—'man at play' is sometimes nicely used as a label for the anthropological background of Cretan art) may well have had a special appeal for the artists of Hatshepsut's court. In many aspects of their work symptoms are apparent of a

new orientation towards femininity and idealism; and particularly in their actual portraits of the Queen (*Ill. 127*) one sees how, in deference to her womanly nature if not to her physical beauty, they have allowed themselves some relaxation of the extreme formality to which sculptors of royal subjects seemed permanently committed.

But this did not mean that greater attention was now paid to the attainment of a physical 'likeness'. The plaster reproduction of an officially approved master-portrait was probably the nearest that an

128 Statue of Tuthmosis III. It is doubtful whether any of these statues are portraits in the modern sense. The aim was rather to present a routine view of the subject in an official style. This statue is typical of the Eighteenth Dynasty: it expresses the benignity and wisdom of the King, as he looks down complacently upon his obedient people

ordinary artist would get to an acquaintance with the physical presence of the Queen. And one notices that, right up to the beginning of the Amarnah period, the portraits of other Pharaohs are still standardized to a point where they become almost indistinguishable. It is the *abstract* qualities of femininity and imperious majesty which are so charmingly combined, for instance in the statue in *Ill. 127*. But the pattern of male statues too is now acquiring a new sort of conventional elegance. In place of the Middle Kingdom autocrats

167

129 A Nubian dancer, from the tomb of Horemheb. The painting here is in a freer convention than usual; it has been suggested that the artist was not fully trained in the accepted methods

who seem to face defiantly perpetual threats of subversion, these New Kingdom figures preside benignly over a political and moral Utopia (e.g. *Ill. 128*).

The second phase of the Eighteenth Dynasty (*Ill. 131–7*) is notable for widespread advances in craftsmanship of all sorts and improvements in the quality of commercial art. Through foreign trade, a profusion of new materials had at this time become available and skilled labour was no longer lacking to convert them into symbols of wealth (*Ill. 131–2*). Diversity of production kept

130 Servants carrying wine-jars and bundles of papyrus from the tomb of Rekh-mi-re at Thebes. The group is remarkable for the skilful designing and placing of the various masses, and for the variety of the movement suggested; there is an alternating rhythm between standing and bending figures. But the draughtsmanship is still in the earlier rather stiff manner, unmodified by the new ideas

pace with the demand for more and more complicated luxuries whose design, as might have been expected, did not unfailingly conform to the highest canons of good taste. Even the production, unprecedented in earlier times, of art-forms with no practical purpose was now stimulated by periodical exhibitions of craftsmanship, sponsored by royalty.

Another change notable at this time is in the development of wall-painting, as seen in the Theban tombs (*Ill. 129–30*). During the early reigns of the New Kingdom, a classical style of painting had

131 Ivory figure of a gazelle. The horns and ears are missing; the desert plants on the base are incised and filled with paste. Ornamental objects with no utilitarian purpose appear for the first time in the early Eighteenth Dynasty

132 Young girl. Ivory. Originally painted—the hair black, the lips red. The unguent-cone on top of the head is pierced, as if the figure were to be suspended. This object again is a mere ornament

been perfected, in which much emphasis was still laid upon the precise drawing of outlines, within which the colour was applied in flat washes on a white or blue-grey background. There was little if any modelling in this painting; no studied suggestion of movement or knowledge of how figures might be multiplied other than by the old *échelon* method. Each group of designs was segregated strictly within the rectangle of the wall which it occupied. By the time the second phase is reached, all this has changed (*Ill. 130*). The brushwork shows signs of a true painter's interest in form as well as outline. Figures are freely and imaginatively grouped or tension between them is created by gesture and movement. The restricting ground-line had already occasionally been dispensed with in the preceding

133 Water-carriers. From the same tomb as the wine-
carriers of *Ill. 130*. The pool in the background (shown in
the plan, though the trees are in profile) illustrates the new
interest in 'landscape'. The figures are grouped with the
intention of showing spatial recession—one man's leg
passes behind a tree. But within their careful outlines the
colour-washes are still flat

136 Two instances of 'cavalier' perspective (i.e. elevated viewpoint): (*above*) from a Mycenaean fresco and (*below*) from a Nineteenth Dynasty Egyptian relief. Compare the attitude of the fallen warrior, and the position of the horse with the scene above

134 Hunting scene from the tomb of User-het. This is the first instance of chariot horses arranged in this curious diagonal stance, which afterwards became widely used in battle scenes. It puts the emphasis on pheno-menal power rather than on speed. The fleeing animals give a vivid impression of movement

135 Last rites before the tomb. Tomb of Neb-Amon. The widow poignantly caresses the feet of the mummy-case in a final gesture of fare-well. For the first time in Egyptian art the ordered ceremony of the funerary ritual cul-minates in the portrayal of actual human grief. The colour is opulent and heraldic

137 Ostrich eggs, ibex, and hare have gained for this little group the evocative label—'Produce of the Desert'

138 (*facing page*) This scene comes from the same series as that in *Ill. 130*. It shows an equally varied pattern of servants' activities, but is less well preserved

phase, and greater freedom thus obtained to express the relative distance of different objects. With the growing interest in the idea of landscape, a sort of multiple horizon is now sometimes substituted for it (*Ill. 133*) and something resembling 'cavalier perspective' adopted to convey a better impression of the terrain in which an event is taking place (*Ill. 136*). Both stages in this development are seen to the best advantage in hunting scenes (*Ill. 134*), where fleeing or pursuing animals appear in violent motion against a background of open country, clearly seen and grasped, though never quite attaining the vivid reality of desert chases in Assyrian reliefs of later times (see *Ill. 167-9*).

Interest in landscape is also evident in the gardens with formal pools (*Ill. 133*), chapels, and even parts of houses, which now appear in paintings for the first time, being subjects perhaps more congenial to the taste of a 'city-dwelling' society than the old rural 'scenes of daily life'. Here again, primitive devices of draughtsmanship are employed to explain the *mise-en-scène*. As for the human figures themselves, these sometimes even turn away from the conventional profile representation and appear full-face. This in turn allows an even more revolutionary departure from tradition, namely

the portrayal of emotion by facial expression as well as gesture (*Ill. 135*). Finally, the first break is now made in the convention of rectangular segregation and designs occasionally extend from wall-to-wall and even from wall-to-ceiling. The statuary of this period tends to follow, with little variation, the principles approved and developed by Hatshepsut's sculptors. However, a taste is now developed for heroic sculpture on a colossal scale, which understandably does not lend itself to naturalistic or 'elegant' treatment. Significant shapes and the choice of appropriate materials become matters of greater significance.

The third of the phases into which the Eighteenth Dynasty has been divided (*Ill. 140–7*) is difficult to assess. The interpretation of the character of the 'Amarnah Revolution' and of the repercussions of Akhenaten's heretical philosophy has been the subject of much controversy, and the only fact about which there has never been any doubt is that the one depended directly upon the other. For the status of an Egyptian Pharaoh and the nature of his relationship with the State render inconceivable any radical change in the national ideology unless directly inspired and personally dictated by the ruler. In fact, Akhenaten's influence on affairs of State is first felt in

139 Tuthmosis III smiting captives, from the temple of
Amon at Karnak. The immortal gesture of conquest, first
seen in the Narmer palette, is here represented on a splendid
scale in sunk relief

the final years of his father's reign, during which he became virtually
co-regent. Thus the first phase in the manifestation of its effects
belongs to the short period directly before and directly after his
actual accession to the throne, during which the court still remained
at Thebes.

Artistically this interlude has a character of its own, appearing to
create an interruption in the development of the 'naturalistic' style
which was begun during the previous reigns and later brought to
perfection during the court's sojourn at Amarnah. It is in itself a

176

140 'Caryatid' statue of King Akhenaten from Karnak. One of thirty such statues erected in the Aten temple during the first years of his sensational apostasy. The Expressionist distortion of form amounts almost to caricature and has no parallel in ancient art

curious phenomenon, but easily understandable if considered as the outcome of a dictated break with tradition, and of a stylistic directive violently at variance with the currently accepted principles of artistic expression. To this phase belong, for instance, the famous 'caryatid' figures from the Aten temple at Karnak (*Ill. 140*), in which one sees aesthetic bewilderment conflicting with a desire to please and producing no more than a caricature. There is no doubt about the source of the directive, since an inscription has survived embodying the explicit statement of a master-sculptor that he was personally instructed by the King. Nor is it surprising that the earliest response to such instruction took so extravagant a form or that the first sculptors who endeavoured to conform to the directive 'lost themselves in the attempt'. It was in the end only the greatest artists who, understanding the potentialities of Akhenaten's approach to 'realism', were able to evolve an acceptable compromise.

By the time the court was established in the new capital, these days of stylistic iconoclasm seem to have been over, and the more extreme mannerisms of the revolutionary period tamed to the requirements of order and sanity. But in art as in all else, the all-pervading influence of the King's personality is still apparent. 'The forces which brought about these artistic changes in Egypt were certainly extraneous to art; this is shown by the abruptness with which new and unprecedented forms appear. It has in fact long ago been realized that the artistic movement of el-Amarnah cannot be separated from the religious reform which led to the foundation of the new capital. The excavator of the site, Sir Flinders Petrie brought the new art into connexion with Akhenaten's insistent claims that the truth must be put before all things. The interpretation is no doubt the right one, but we must be careful to determine exactly what we mean by truth in this context. The truth at which Akhenaten was aiming was, at least in the sphere of art, truth of a very particular and limited kind, the subjective truth of the senses; it was characteristic of Akhenaten's self-centred nature that he ignored the objective universal truth which the traditional formal language of Egyptian art had tried to express. . . . In the sphere of religion likewise he pretended to restore primeval truth overgrown by ritual and

141 A feast, from the tomb of Nakht, at Thebes. In his striving towards naturalism the artist has here endeavoured to capture the passing impressions of casual inter-course. Groups of guests and dancers are connected by gesture as well as by actual contact. The sudden movement of a girl in the foreground reveals a frontal view of her left breast—a striking departure from earlier convention

formalistic dogma, while he did nothing more than force the elevated conclusions of his personal reflections on a perplexed population.' Petrie's early impressions of Amarnah art have thus been most explicitly qualified by Frankfort.

We see then in the art of Amarnah the logical development of a distinctive style, temporarily side-tracked in an endeavour to express the ideological aberrations of a single individual (e.g. *Ill. 140*). Still surviving and even accentuated, is the 'naturalism' at which it originally aimed. In wall-painting, landscape has become a subject of study in its own right, as one understands for instance from the frescoes in the 'North Palace' at Amarnah (*Ill. 145*), where the behaviour and appearance of birds and animals is affectionately observed. Here, too, an even closer approach to perspective is achieved by the use of new devices such as diagonal paths to suggest receding distance in a garden scene, and there is no longer any hesitation in spreading a composition over adjoining walls. Human figures are grouped together in intelligible patterns or related to each other by gestures of

142 Sculptor's model relief, used in the workshop as a pattern—official portraits of the royal family, presumably Akhenaten and Nofretiti

143 Detail of a relief from the tomb of the vizier Ramose. The subtle modelling of the face is beautifully contrasted with the conventional texture of the hair to produce a design without rival in the relief-carving of any other period

144 Portrait-bust of Queen Nofretiti. Part of a composite statue, and probably the most famous of Egyptian antiquities. Only the imagination of an Amarnah artist could have produced this idealized portrait of Akhenaten's wife

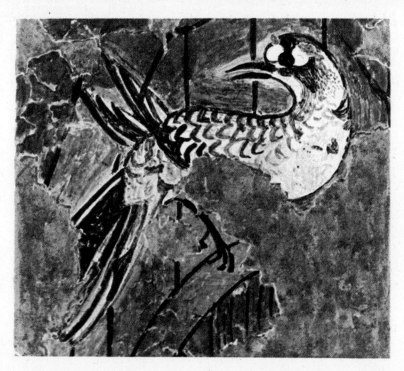

145 A shrike in the marshes. One of the rooms of the 'North Palace' at Tell-el-Amarnah was decorated with a continuous scene of bird life. Here we can see a departure from linear conventions and a design built up from brush-strokes

remarkable subtlety and understanding. The same naturalism appears in a rather more idealized form in the interesting 'workshop' figures from sculptors' studios—mostly portraits of the royal family (*Ill. 142*). But superimposed upon all this, in a form now happily modified, are the symbols of Akhenaten's revolutionary ideology, reminding one of his passion for 'actuality'—for the visual representation of things as they are, as opposed to the conceptual portrayal of how they should be. In the 'conversation pieces' depicting the King in a domestic setting so much sentimentality is to be found that their effect is one of cloying sweetness (*Ill. 146*). Their composition, too, is mismanaged, because nothing short of perspective could

146 Relief-carving of Akhenaten and his family, illustrating what critics have called the 'cloying naturalism' of late Amarnah art. The group is held together by the children's gestures as well as by the rays of the Aten sun-disk

adequately have met its practical requirements. And perspective was still unknown.

In her book *Arrest and Movement* Mrs H. A. G. Frankfort beautifully evokes the philosophical climate in Amarnah. 'In the strangely artificial town, built, after the religious and political schism, on clean desert soil, communal life was not only cut off from the burden of tradition, but also from its perennial values. It was, in all appearances, a gay uprooted irresponsible existence to which only the religious awareness of the beauty of life, expressed and fostered by the king, gave a kind of frail dignity and grace. This surely was the strangest effort ever made to live by the affirmation of joy and beauty alone, an artificial holiday which, if it was not to end in a kind of aesthetic dissipation, was bound to end in disaster. There is actually

147 Head of Nofretiti. This time the portrait is unfinished, and we are not distracted
from the modelling by the paint (cf. *Ill. 144*). A close-fitting wig of faience
would have been attached to the upper part; the eyes would have been painted in

148 Tutelary goddesses from the tomb of Tut-ankh-amon: Neith, Isis, and Selkit. Each has a distinguishing symbol on her head, and is clad in a tight-fitting pleated garment tied at the waist. The eyes are painted

some evidence that it did both before it faded out, leaving few traces in a period of renewed acceptance of traditional values.'

The fourth and last phase of the Eighteenth Dynasty—the aftermath of the Amarnah experiment—is best known artistically from the contents of Tut-ankh-amon's tomb (*Ill. 148-9*). His short reign saw the beginnings of a return to orthodoxy; the rejection of the Aten-cult and the rehabilitation of Amen at Thebes. Yet among the opulent furnishings of his tomb, the aroma of artistic heresy is still unmistakable. Akhenaten had suffered from an uncommon but recognized disease which resulted in the deformation of skull and

149 Golden throne of Tut-ankh-amon. The back panel, of wood overlaid with gold, silver, and inlays, shows the King in a pavilion preparing for some important ceremony. It is one of the most outstanding examples of fine craftsmanship which have survived from antiquity

hips. This disfiguration created a fashion in outline, which can still be recognized in the figures of goddesses in gilded wood, guarding Tut-ankh-amon's inner shrine—surely some of the most exquisite products of Egyptian sensibility—and though these and other items are now thought to have been made in the reign of Tut-ankh-amon's predecessor, they would hardly have been tolerated if reaction against the symbols of apostasy had yet been strongly felt. But strangely enough, it is not until the reign of Horemheb, when the reaction was complete and all political traces of the revolution eliminated, that relief-sculptures in his and other Memphite tombs show the ultimately successful synthesis of experiment and tradition that had been achieved.

The cycle of art-history in the Eighteenth Dynasty is thus completed, and its completion also brings the tide of progressive creation in Egyptian art to a high-water-mark from which it must inevitably recede. During the Nineteenth and Twentieth Dynasties, which bring to an end the history of the New Kingdom, it reverted to the broad stream of traditional conservatism. The palace régime in these days had changed somewhat in character owing to the fact that the royal family was now of Lower Egyptian extraction. When therefore it became necessary for Ramesses I to find a more accessible political centre from which the Mediterranean territories reconquered by Horemheb might be administered and safeguarded, it seemed natural to him to establish a new State-capital at the old Hyksos stronghold at Tanis-Avaris. Thebes, however, retained its position as the cultural and religious centre of national life. Kings continued to build themselves vaster and more grandiose temples in southern religious centres such as Luxor, Karnak, or Abydos, and to be buried among the Theban hills. But in relief-carving and wall-paintings (*Ill. 150*), though technical accomplishment remained undiminished, the glory of creative invention had departed, and mere elegance of style could no longer disguise the sterile repetition of conventional motifs. Evidence of this can already be seen for instance in the paintings from Ramesside tombs, and in the celebrated cycle of reliefs so perfectly preserved in the funerary temple of Sethos I at Abydos (*Ill. 151–2*). And finally, as an example of the concluding phase of artistic development in dynastic times when a king's memorial ambition could find no better expression than in exaggeration by some purely technical *tour de force*, there is the great temple at Abu Simbel in southern Nubia, which Ramesses II preferred to carve out of the solid rock rather than build on any of the fine open sites which offered themselves (*Ill. 153*). The four royal statues, more than forty feet high, ornamenting the façade, symbolize the culminating-point in the age-long development of a cardinal theme in Egyptian art, beyond which to contrive yet other variations would no longer have been profitable.

150 Painting from the tomb of User-het. A formal portrait of the tomb-owner's wife and mother. Above them is a conventionalized fig tree laden with fruit. They wear broad collars of faience beads and head-bands. On their long wigs are the usual cones of myrrh (cf. *Ill. 123*)

151 (*above*) Sethos I as Osiris with the god Thoth, from his temple at Abydos. The ibis-headed god offers the *ankh*, symbol of life, to Sethos, who carries a crook-shaped sceptre. In his left hand Thoth carries the plant emblems, entwined with cobras, of Upper and Lower Egypt

←
152 (*left*) The goddess Isis, from the same temple. She wears a vulture hood and a head-dress encircled with cobras. Aesthetically this final stage of Egyptian art shows elegance rather than inspiration

153 Colossi of the Great Temple at Abu Simbel (Ramesses II). The four statues of kings are more than forty feet high. Behind them the complex of halls and chambers actually composing a funerary temple is carved into the solid rock. The sheer scale creates an overwhelming impression but cannot disguise the lack of inspiration. The technical qualities have become coarser

192

PART SIX

Assyrian and Iron Age Art

At a very early stage in Mesopotamian history, the city of Assur on the Middle Tigris gave its name to a small Sumerian State, and from the eighteenth century B.C. onwards, something is known of its history. But it was not until about 1350 B.C., when Babylonia was weakened by Kassite domination and Mitanni by pressure from the Hittites, that Assyria was able to assert its independence and extend its frontiers. Historically, the remainder of the second millennium B.C. is known as the Middle Assyrian period and that from 1000 B.C. till the fall of Nineveh in 612 B.C. as Late Assyrian.

Unfortunately little has survived by which Middle Assyrian art can be judged: only in contemporary cylinder-seals is it possible to detect the first sign of individual character, markedly different from the exhausted formalism of Kassite and Mitannian glyptic. Already conspicuous is the seal-cutter's purely secular interest in wild animals and landscape and the capacity for imparting vitality to both which became so notable a feature of Assyrian art in later times. Even the conventional arrangement of opposed beasts had begun to lose its heraldic character (*Ill. 154*). Late Assyrian art on the other hand is represented by so prodigious a volume of sculptured material, that only its remarkable consistency of style and content makes it possible to discuss in general terms. Its history is mainly the history of relief-carving; for, though statues in the round do exist, those which are not, like the beautiful amber figure at Boston (*Ill. 155*), small enough to be considered as jewellers' work suggest by their ineptitude that this was not a form of expression which came at all naturally to Assyrian sculptors. The portal-sculptures (*Ill. 156*), which must be thought of by many as the most characteristically Assyrian art-form, do not in fact fall into this category at all. They are really no more than 'double-aspect' reliefs, and have their origin (for all we know to

154 Middle Assyrian cylinder-seal—stag and trees. Amidst the decadent formalism of Kassite and Mitannian glyptic the first purely Assyrian products show individual vitality: a non-heraldic interest in animals and the observation of landscape

the contrary) in a Hittite invention of the fourteenth century B.C. (*Ill. 182*).

The Assyrians first began to adorn the walls of their palaces with reliefs early in the ninth century, when Assurnasirpal II moved the capital from Assur itself to Nimrud (Caleh) on the left bank of the Tigris. It seems possible that this was a genuine innovation, for till then the only comparable form of ornament in Mesopotamia had been the processions of rather squat figures painted along the base of the walls in Kassite palaces, as for instance at Dur Kurigalzu. The earliest group of reliefs then, is derived from excavations at Nimrud and date from the reigns of Assurnasirpal II and his son Shalmaneser III in the first quarter of the ninth century B.C. (*Ill. 157, 161, 162*). Another group comes from Khorsabad (Dur Sharrukim) where Sargon II established a short-lived capital (rather like that of Akhenaten at Amarnah) in the second half of the eighth century (*Ill. 163*). The third group comes from the palaces of Nineveh which, after Sargon's venture at Khorsabad had been abandoned, was largely rebuilt by Sennacherib and Assurbanipal (*Ill. 160, 164–9*). The reliefs are used exclusively to decorate the interior of buildings, and are designed to form a continuous frieze around the walls of halls and chambers. In the early days they were usually about seven feet high,

155 Assyrian statues in the round are extremely rare, and this figure, which is less than a foot high, of amber and ornamented with a gold setting for precious stones, if genuine, must be treated as goldsmith's work. It is also unusual for an Assyrian king to be depicted with his hands folded in the ritual gesture of prayer

with the design occasionally arranged in two superimposed registers with a band of cuneiform inscription between. But in later buildings, as for instance in Sargon's palace at Khorsabad, the individual sculptured figures reached a height of nine feet. The subjects generally chosen for the designs show little interest in religious matters. This has given place to a straightforward glorification of the King himself, either by scenes of ceremonial homage or by prolonged pictorial narratives of his achievements. In the more heraldic groups, miscellaneous monsters with a protective purpose do occasionally appear, as well as benevolent winged beings, usually referred to as 'genii'. But the form of an actual god rarely appears unless it be the ever-present figure of Assur himself, enshrined with his bow in a winged sun-disk.

The most oft-repeated, though never quite monotonous, subjects of the reliefs are detailed scenes of military conquest and the ruthless

157 King Assurnasirpal, victorious in battle, is a central
theme in the narrative relief-sculptures which adorn his
palace at Nimrud. As is usual in Assyrian reliefs, the King
is of normal stature and, unlike the invulnerable royal
figures in Egyptian battle scenes, dangerously exposed to
the arrows of enemy archers

suppression of revolt in disaffected provinces or dependencies. The
Assyrian army prepares for war; led by the King it crosses difficult
country on the way to attack a walled city, probably among mountains: the city is taken, burnt, and demolished; the enemy leaders are
punished with ingenious brutality; a victory is then celebrated. In
the inscriptions the outcome of a minor campaign of this sort is
recorded by the laconic comment, 'So I came upon them and destroyed them utterly and turned their cities into forgotten mounds.'
It has been suggested that Assyrian sculptors learnt something from
the reliefs of the Egyptian New Kingdom. Probable as this may
seem (since the latter had for the most part already been in existence
for five centuries), differences of approach to the actual purpose of the
designs are no less conspicuous than contrasting qualities of style.
There is no question of the Assyrian sculptures being dedicated to
any magic or religious function: they are mere records of profane

197

158 Another relief from Nimrud, showing an attack on a walled city. The attacking Assyrians are crossing a river on inflated skins, as is often done today in Iraq. The vertical depth of the river-bank is suggested, thus giving a stereoscopic effect to the picture

events directed to a temporal end. For this reason the figure of the King, for instance, is never distinguished by disproportionate size. His stature is no more than human. Nor does one find in the battle scenes that which in the Egyptian reliefs has been called 'the timeless assertion of inevitable royal victory'. The scenes themselves are often arranged episodically—that is, they represent successive developments in the progress of a single action—and if one examines them in detail one sees that at no time is the over-all outcome anticipated. The King himself in his chariot is in obvious danger from enemy archers, from whom at times he appears most inadequately protected (*Ill. 157*).

But what above all distinguishes the Assyrian sculptures is their stylistic vitality and fanciful detail. Horses in particular are drawn with great understanding and expression (*Ill. 167*); even their movements in swimming seem the result of close observation.

159 Reconstruction of a wall-painting from a chamber in Sargon II's citadel at Khorsabad. Beneath the painting would have been a line of sculptured stone slabs. The bright, almost garish, colours, would have been modified by the subdued light which reached the throne-room through the open doors only

160 Reliefs of Sennacherib from Nineveh. A scene in the strange landscape of the South Mesopotamian marshes, where Assyrian soldiers seek out the rebel marsh-dwellers, is strikingly conveyed

Those drawing chariots are not thrown upwards diagonally in a stylized prance but conform realistically to the horizontal limitations of the frieze. Interest, too, in the relationship in space of figures composing a scene had much increased (*Ill. 165*). Already in the Nimrud reliefs one sees the stereoscopic effect obtained when a river-bank is given vertical depth (*Ill. 158*), or how the placing of figures in a void without groundlines can suggest the idea of relative distance (*Ill. 169*).

Some of these qualities are again in evidence during the reign of Shalmaneser III, which saw a new and very striking development in architectural ornament, namely relief-modelling in metal. The huge wooden gates of a palace at Balawat, near Nimrud, were decorated with horizontal bands of bronze, eleven inches deep, each modelled by a *repoussé* process with a double register of narrative scenes (*Ill. 161*). The artistic quality of the designs shows no particular distinction, but they give an impression of great animation and the modelling is technically excellent. Like the relief-sculptors, these metal-workers were concerned with the episodic rendering of

historical subjects, and the limitations imposed on them by the narrow dimensions of the registers naturally made them prefer those most easily treated as a procession. Less frequently static scenes do occur, and great ingenuity has then to be used in giving reality to a landscape. The artist has in this case been compelled to fall back on traditional formulae for suggesting features such as a river and a range of mountains.

Chronologically, the next development in Assyrian art is a short interlude under Tiglathpilesar III, when poverty of resources caused a return to the practice of wall-painting in place of relief-carving. A palace at Til Barsip on the Middle Euphrates was decorated with rather clumsily designed frescoes. When reliefs appear again in the time of King Sargon II, they are on a grandiose scale, suitable to the magnitude of his enterprise in founding a new State-capital at Khorsabad north of Nineveh. The carving of narrative and historical subjects has now largely been abandoned, and is replaced by the more tedious symbols of pomp and ceremony. In the great elevated palace at Khorsabad, destroyed and abandoned almost before it had been officially occupied, communicating-halls and ante-rooms are decorated with processions of stiffly arranged figures, often now occupying the full height of a stone dado which had increased to nearly nine feet. Separated by the great portal-sculptures of winged bulls and genii, files of courtiers, officials, and servants standimm obilized in the routine of ceremonial homage to the King's secular majesty. Their stereotyped profiles are repeated with the same impersonal monotony as in the Til Barsip paintings, and despite some improvement in the quality of carving the general effect lacks any vestige of real elegance. In the smaller chambers more latitude

161 Bronze relief from the 'Balawat Gates'. The scenes are arranged in bands only five inches high, first engraved and then embossed by hammering from behind. In the top register Tyre, from its island, sends tribute to the Assyrians; at the bottom are Assyrian officers in chariots

has been allowed to the artist and there is occasionally a hunting scene (*Ill. 163*), or, in one rare case, the pictorial record of a sea battle. However, the monotony of the processional scene is occasionally relieved by the sparing use of pigment on the reliefs. There are traces of a warm flesh-tint and black paint on hair and beards.

Evidence of much ornament other than sculpture is to be found among the Sargonid buildings. Some major chambers in the Khorsabad citadel were adorned with a formal scheme of decoration (*Ill. 159*) painted in elementary colours over a white ground on the mud-plaster surface of the walls. Temples of the same period had

162 Reliefs of Assurnasirpal. Two chariots, each drawn by four horses, are shown behind each other. Details are rendered with vividness and variety even when the subjects are the same

the base of their façades embellished with panels of glazed bricks, depicting in colour mythological animals and other religious symbols. Threshold-slabs, particularly in these temples, are decorated in relief with formal patterns clearly intended to represent woven floor-coverings. Reproductions of more elaborate weaving and embroidery are also to be seen in the engraving of royal garments in the relief-sculptures, and the Assyrians are known to have excelled in this craft as the inhabitants of Mosul did in a later age.

There remain two more notable groups of Assyrian reliefs—both from buildings on the major palace-mound, Küyünjik, at Nineveh. One comes from the palace of Sennacherib and dates from the time when he rebuilt the city after Sargon's death and the failure of the

163 Hunting scene, from Khorsabad. Characteristically, more attention is paid to the drawing of animals and birds than to the human figures. A hare is among the trophies carried home

Khorsabad experiment (*Ill. 160*). The other belongs to the time of his son, Assurbanipal (*Ill. 164–9*). The sculptors of Sennacherib's time returned with unmistakable zest to the narrative and documentary subjects of the pre-Sargonid period. They brought a new ingenuity to bear on the rendering of complicated action and the characteristic details of the landscapes in which it took place. Sometimes their efforts were remarkably successful, particularly when attention was paid to the studied composition of contrasting sculptural textures. This is best seen in the narrative of a campaign fought by Sennacherib in the famous marsh-country at the junction of the Tigris and Euphrates (*Ill. 160*) (which has for the first time been sensitively described in a recently published travel-book) and it is

suggest recession in the line of approach towards the walls has created chaos in the composition. This device was afterwards discarded

most interesting to compare with the Egyptian rendering of events in a similar setting where the textural patterns used for instance to signify water, have the same meaning. Sometimes, however, the results were less satisfying. The full height of the slabs had once more been brought into use in order to obtain space for larger and more elaborate pictures (*Ill. 164–5*); and one sees successive attempts, each more misguided than the last, to convey essential impressions of distance and space-relationship, which a few centuries later would have presented little difficulty. The attempt to use diagonal lines for this purpose ended in a form of frustration which can also be seen in Assurbanipal's palace (*Ill. 164*).

Among the sculptures of Assurbanipal's time there is evidence of greater restraint in the struggle for pictorial expression (*Ill. 166–9*).

165 The defeat of the Elamites from Sennacherib's palace at Nineveh. This is a detail from a highly complicated scene, showing incidents in a battle. Corpses of the King's enemies lie on every side among the conveniently drawn trees

In the narrative scenes, the use of multiple registers is once more in order, and when diagonals occur they are used with so much subtlety that some critics are inclined to detect in them the first elements of true perspective (*Ill. 166*). But the most remarkable contribution to the perfection of contemporary design made during this reign, was in another milieu. Even in the life of an Assyrian king, there must have been occasional periods of military inactivity, and during these, the hunting of wild animals was substituted as a suitably masculine occupation. And here the Assyrian relief-sculptors found a subject entirely to their liking. The 'Lion Hunt' carvings from Assurbanipal's palace (*Ill. 167–9*) are perhaps the best known of all their works. They reveal many remarkable qualities—dramatic composition—close, and even affectionate observation of characteristic

207

166 A scene from Assurbanipal's palace, showing the capture of a city. At the top, fortifications are being demolished; and below, the looting soldiers leave the gate by a road, shown by two lines which widen towards the spectator, suggesting the beginning of perspective

167 Part of the Assurbanipal 'Lion Hunt' sequence. This marks the culmination of Assyrian relief-sculpture; in the portrayal of animals in violent movement it has never been surpassed. The occasional projection of the carving beyond the limits of the frieze gives an extra sense of urgent vitality to the design

form or gesture—vivid rendering of violent action—and so forth. But to anyone familiar with the desert background against which these episodes are enacted, the central accomplishment amounting to an artistic *tour de force* is the rendering of a featureless landscape by no other means than the studied spacing of the figures (*Ill. 169*). The expression of more abstract situations as for instance the poignant quandary of a mare whose flight is impeded by the presence of her foal—a general understanding of animal suffering, capable of 'raising these scenes to the stature of a tragedy', suggests a degree of sensibility with which one almost hesitates to credit Assyrian artists. There is a secondary convention in Assyrian relief-carving which is applied to monumental devices carved on the vertical faces of rocks in suitable localities (Bavian, Maltai, etc.) to commemorate historical events; but this is heraldic and formal, with

168 (*above*) A dying lion. Extraordinary subtlety of observation is combined with pathos. 'The lion's force is suddenly broken, the huge paws are paralysed. The snarl stiffens, and in a moment the heavy body will sink to the ground.' (Frankfort)

169 (*below*) Wild asses hunted with mastiffs. The mare's flight is hampered by thoughts of her foal

170 Painted ivory head from Nimrud. Eyes and eyebrows were originally inlaid
and pendants round the neck encrusted with gold

171 Bronze bowl from Nimrud. A number of such bowls have been found, but there has been a dispute over their place of origin. Patterns range from purely geometric, as here, to mythological scenes

no aspiration towards abstract meaning beyond the simple expression of monumentality. They in fact resemble on a colossal scale the designs on Late Assyrian cylinder-seals, whose main virtue in turn lies in the competence of their miniature rendering.

Finally, there are the ivory carvings used during the eighth and seventh centuries to adorn court furniture, though neither in design nor craftsmanship can they be said to be truly Assyrian. High society in Assyria was by this time distinctly cosmopolitan and the unique skill of foreign workmen in certain materials made the importation of their products or their own employment fashionable.

172 Another bronze bowl from Nimrud; this is unusual in its use of Egyptian motifs—winged scarabs and falcon-headed sphinxes trampling on enemies. The geometric centre design, however, is quite un-Egyptian

To this we owe some fine examples of Phoenician bronze (*Ill. 171–2*) and above all the great and varied collection of delicate ivory carvings (*Ill. 173*) whose decorative motifs would have appeared so much more at home in Damascus, Tyre, or Sidon, or even in Egypt from which the art of the Syrian cities was ultimately derived. Female figures are for instance frequently portrayed, contrary to Assyrian convention. Themselves exquisitely modelled, the reliefs were as a rule heavily encrusted with gold-foil and further enriched with *cloisonné* inlays of lapis-lazuli and crimson paste; and one can well understand that the Assyrians appreciated their elegance.

To the north and west of Assyria, in the Levant and among the Taurus Mountains, obscurer peoples produced less pretentious works of art during this period. The Anatolian plateau was now occupied by the Phrygians, who in the final centuries of the second millennium B.C., had driven the imperial Hittites from their homeland in the Halys country. But, during the ninth and eighth centuries, in a scattered pattern of walled cities, extending from Malatya in the north to Carchemish on the Euphrates and Hama in the Orontes Valley, a strange aftermath of Hittite history was played out during the ninth and eighth centuries. The art of these cities is known by courtesy as 'Hittite', because it is associated with the earlier insignia of Hittite culture, including the hieroglyph writing of the Luvian language. But it is, in fact, a complicated hybrid—as complicated, for instance, as the remnants of British culture would be, if its preservation were suddenly restricted to a territory with a predominantly French-Canadian population. In a city like Carchemish, expatriate Hittites rubbed shoulders with Phoenicians, Hurrians, and tribal Aramaeans; and as the cities came with increasing frequency to be subjected to Assyrian domination, all traces of individuality in their culture were eventually swamped by foreign influence.

Yet there are interesting features among the surviving monuments. The city of Malatya remained sufficiently remote from both Syria and Mesopotamia to have retained some sculptors still familiar with the Hittite tradition which had its roots in Boghazköy. Reliefs from a ninth-century gateway at Malatya in addition to their archaeological interest have some pretention to good craftsmanship (*Ill. 178*) and there is a striking portrait-statue of a king, about twice life-size (*Ill. 177*). At Ivriz, too, on the northern flank of Taurus, a really magnificent rock-relief whose subject is self-explanatory (*Ill. 181*) when one understands its situation at the source of a life-giving

→

173 Ethiopian slain by a lion. One of the masterpieces of the Nimrud ivories, Phoenician in inspiration, if not in workmanship. 'In spite of the loss of the greater part of the gold overlay and blue and red incrustations, this ornament still gives the effect of a faceted polychrome jewel.' (Mallowan)

174 (*above*) Side of an ivory box from the 'Treasure of Ziwiye'.
A contrasting style of carving from Azerbaijan

175 (*right*) Ivory panel from Nimrud showing obvious Egyptian
influence. Two divine attendants greet with upraised arms a
cartouche containing the name of an unknown prince

176 Ivory openwork plaque showing a lion in a lily grove and facing a sacred tree. The lion has a head-dress and breastplate copied from the Egyptian goddess Hathor

177 Colossal statue of a king, fro Malatya. A striking portrait-statue, abo twice life-size, stylistically related more Assyria than to Anatolia

178 Relief from a ninth-century gateway at Malatya. The art of Malatya represents a late survival of the Hittite tradition, and there are already signs of provincialism in this relief

torrent of water, makes little concession to the stylistic conventions of neighbouring countries. At other sites sculpture in the round is represented both by statues and column-bases supported on paired animals (*Ill. 179*). Grotesque examples of such portal-figures were found in a palace at Tell Halaf (*Ill. 180*) which owed its unique character to local rulers of predominantly Aramaean (Arab) extraction.

But by far the most plentiful relics of the 'Neo-Hittite' or 'Syro-Hittite' culture are the sculptured 'orthostats'—slabs of stone set up side by side, to protect and adorn the bases of walls in public buildings. Apart from Carchemish (*Ill. 183, 189*) they were to be seen at Sinjerli, Sakjegözi, Marash, and many other cities, crudely carved with stiff and repetitive figures and scenes—an art initially hampered by choice of material, which was often intractable basalt, alternating in a manner most disturbing to the eye with slabs of coarse limestone. Perhaps aesthetically the least attractive of all are the reliefs which accompanied the now-famous bilingual inscription written in 'Hittite' and Phoenician, in the little 'country-palace' at Karatepe in northern Cilicia (*Ill. 184–5*). Here, side by side, one may see slabs of uneven size bearing reliefs which may be successively identified as Phoenician, Assyrian, and even Egyptian in style and symbolism.

179 Statue of a god-king on a square throne from Carchemish. The base with two lions is of the type used at the time to support columns

180 'Caryatid' figure from Tell Halaf. Three of these huge and unattractive statues, mounted on sculptured animals, supported the roof of a portico in front of the palace

181 Rock-relief at Ivriz. This carving above the source of a
river is an expression of gratitude to the god for agricultural
abundance. The King, whose name is given, was a vassal of
Assyria, whence the sculptor partly derived his style

182 One of a pair of sculptured sphinxes from Alaca Hüyük, which occupied a position similar to the winged bulls at Khorsabad (*Ill. 156*). There is Egyptian influence in such features as the head-dress

183 Relief from Carchemish. Basalt is an awkward stone to carve, and one misses the Assyrian gift for drawing animals. Like other Hittite sculpture, this gives one an impression of over-confident ineptitude

Flourishing in the ninth and eighth centuries B.C., contemporaneously with the Syro-Hittite States, was the Kingdom of Urartu, centred upon Lake Van. Urartian art is perhaps derivatively too closely related to that of Assyria to merit more than a casual reference here. But it seems to have inspired a school of metal-workers, whose influence enlivened the minor arts of neighbouring countries over a long period of time. In an Urartian temple, depicted in an Assyrian relief at Khorsabad, high bronze cauldrons supported by iron tripods are to be seen; and identical vessels, their rims decorated with finely modelled bulls' heads, have been dug up at an Urartian site near

184 A relief from Karatepe showing birds of prey and a human figure between beasts in the Mesopotamian manner

185 Like that on the left, this relief with its crude synthesis of foreign styles, accompanied the famous bilingual inscription

Erzinjan. More recently two more examples have been found in the great tumulus burial known as the 'Tomb of Midas' at Gordium in Phrygia; and these are surprisingly decorated with the so-called 'siren' heads which reappear a little later in Greece. In another Sargonid relief, court attendants carry the bucket-shaped bronze vessel known as a *situla*, modelled in the shape of a lion's head. These striking objects were known to be of Urartian origin, but in this case it remained for the Gordium tombs to provide the first surviving examples, perfectly preserved (*Ill. 186*).

225

186 Bronze *situla* in the shape of a lion's head from Gordium. The eyes are inlaid with white paste and blue stone. Objects like this are represented in Assyrian reliefs of the time of Sargon II

The Gordium tombs have also provided the most outstanding examples of purely Phrygian art—elaborate furniture, finely carved and inlaid with rare woods; moulded vessels in clear glass and magnificent pottery with designs in several colours (*Ill. 187*). Beyond this, what little is known of Phrygian craftsmanship is mainly in the sphere of architectural terracottas (*Ill. 188*); and rock-monuments, sculptured to resemble the façades of buildings, give some indication of the position in which they were placed. For the rest Phrygian culture has so Western a flavour that its products are out of harmony with those of the countries we are considering.

187 Group of Phrygian painted vessels from the 'Child's Tumulus' at Gordium. Magnificent though comic pottery, with designs in several colours

188 Phrygian terracotta-reliefs. The use of terracotta for architectural ornament was an innovation of this time. The design recalls those on earlier cylinder-seals

189 Relief from Carchemish. Wall-ornaments copied from those of Assyria without the requisite knowledge of design and craftsmanship. All Syro–Hittite art has this same provincial quality in relation to that of Mesopotamia and Egypt

PART SEVEN

Late Babylonian and Persian Art

Some years before the final fall of Nineveh, a new dynasty was founded in the old South Mesopotamian capital at Babylon. It lasted less than a century, but during this period a tremendous revival of economic prosperity took place and was accompanied by a final flowering of Mesopotamian culture. Even more notable was a sudden burst of architectural activity and invention on a scale greater than anything hitherto attempted. During the reigns of Nabopolassar and his son, Nebuchadnezzar, temples and *ziggurats* were repaired and rebuilt in almost all the old dynastic cities, while Babylon itself became the vast and sophisticated metropolis, against which the Old Testament prophets directed the bitter invective of their exile. In spite of the ultimate destruction, which they correctly predicted for the great city, it is upon the surviving remains of buildings dating from this period that we have to rely in forming any judgment at all about the character of Neo-Babylonian art. For here, even more than in the earlier context, we are struck by the paradoxical failure of archaeological research to produce any considerable works of art other than those related to architecture. Nevertheless, the little which has in fact been recovered does show that, so far from being a prolongation of Assyrian culture this was a veritable revival or culmination of the age-old South Meso-potamian traditions which had been largely in abeyance since the collapse of the Kassite dynasty late in the second millennium.

For this conclusion then, our evidence is limited for the most part to the ornament with which the façades of mud-brick buildings were adorned by architects deprived of any more distinguished material than alluvial clay. In the city itself, the most grandiose architectural effect was contrived by the disposal of the principal public buildings along a wide 'Procession Street', which led through the centre of the town to the main temple-enclosure, Etemenanki

190 A bull from the 'Ishtar Gate', Babylon. Each individual figure was modelled on a rectangular panel of clay; cut up into separate bricks while still soft; then glazed, fired, and reassembled on the façade

and Marduk's *ziggurat* ('The Tower of Babel'). Where it passed through the inner city-wall, the pylons of the famous 'Ishtar Gate' and the crenellated walls flanking the street itself, were ornamented with glazed bricks, in which huge figures of bulls and dragons were depicted in bright colours—brown, white, and yellow on a blue ground (*Ill. 190–1*). But where the figures on the glazed-brick façades of Assyrian buildings were produced by flat, under-glaze painting, these in Babylon were modelled in sharp relief. Nor were they necessarily arranged to face towards the approaching visitor, as the guardian figures of Assyrian doorways were made to do; instead they were simply and rather artlessly distributed over the façade. On the outside wall of Nebuchadnezzar's throne-room, this form of decoration received a more coherent treatment—a pattern of slender masts with volute and palmette terminal ornament were connected by pendant garlands of flowers, once more rendered in white and yellow against a blue background.

191 The reconstructed 'Ishtar Gate', Babylon. The animals—bulls and dragons—
are the conventional heraldic figures of the time. The whole gateway formed a
splendid polychrome composition

For the rest, our entire knowledge of the works of art of Nebuchadnezzar's Babylon depends upon no more than a dozen handfuls of cylinder-seals (*Ill. 192*) and a number of indifferently modelled terracottas. If archaeology had not provided documentary evidence to the contrary, one might have been excused for suspecting the glories of Neo-Babylonia of being comparable with those of the 'Empire of Trebizond', which are said to have 'existed only in the imagination of the most credulous historians'.

It was in Nebuchadnezzar's throne-room that the last Babylonian king Nabonidus (or according to the Biblical legend, Belshazzar), saw the doom of his country forecast in the 'Writing on the Wall'. Cyrus, the first Achaemenid ruler of Persia, who in fact caused its downfall, had been a vassal of the Medes who destroyed Nineveh eighty years earlier: but his defeat in rapid succession of his Median overlord, Astyages, of the Lydian king, Croesus, and finally of Nabonidus, inaugurated a new era, during which the whole of the Near East came to be ruled from the Persian capital at Persepolis. At this point a few words become necessary regarding the earlier history of those lands which we now know as Iran.

Curiously enough, actual events in Iran during the third and second millennia B.C. are known only from the written records of neighbouring Mesopotamia: and indeed, it is only in regard to those districts of modern Iran which are immediately adjacent to its south-west frontier with Iraq (in ancient times, Elam, with its capital at Susa, and the tribal peoples of the Zagros area, Guti and Lullabi), that anything is known at all. As for these latter, their history may indeed be summarized in a few words. The character and art of the Lullabi are known from references in the Akkadian records to trade or periodical hostilities, and from a rock-relief in which the style and composition of Naram-Sin's famous stela are crudely imitated. The Guti we have already seen devastating southern Iraq, and interrupting the dynastic sequence in every Mesopotamian State except Lagash. Elam, on the other hand, seems to have profited from a more politically continuous and culturally progressive existence during the Bronze Age, though this also can be inferred only from extraneous records. During wars fought by

192 Neo-Babylonian cylinder-seal, showing a priest worshipping not the effigies of gods, but their symbols as they appeared mounted on stands in the temple

Elamite kings against the Mesopotamian cities, famous sculptures, including the stela of Hammurabi itself, were carried away as booty to Susa and served as models for an increasingly distinguished school of Iranian artists. At Choga Zambil, near the capital, the structure of a large and well-designed *ziggurat* temple has recently been brought to light.

From about 1000 B.C. onwards, Indo-European peoples migrated southward into Iran. Scythians from South Russia, Cimmerians from the Caucasus, Medes and Persians from Central Asia, all in turn overran the highlands overlooking Mesopotamia, until even Elam succumbed and ceased to exist as a political entity. But even before this happened, in the late second millennium, one strange isolated repository of Iranian art and craftsmanship had begun to accumulate in the deep valleys between the Zagros ranges. This was the complex of Late Bronze and Iron Age cemeteries, which in our own time became the source of the so-called 'Luristan Bronzes' (*Ill. 193–200*).

Between the years 1930 and 1934, the Luristan cemeteries were
excavated by Persians commercially interested in the sale of
antiquities, who consequently did not encourage the competition
of qualified archaeologists. The burials were in shallow, stone-lined
graves, often actually visible above the surface; and in the course of
those years between four and five hundred burial-grounds appear
to have been rifled, each of them comprising about two hundred
graves. The graves contained a little pottery and glass, a few stone
objects, and a vast quantity of ornamental bronzes, all of which soon
appeared in museums or on the market, and created a considerable
stir. First estimates for the date of the burials varied by as much as
two thousand years: and further study has since revealed that they
must indeed cover a fairly long period of time. Comparison with
metal types, found for instance at Tepe Ghiyan and Sialk, has

193 Heads of two Luristan pins. These represent an Iranian culture which is known only from the contents of graves

established one group as belonging to the later half of the second millennium B.C., while other objects clearly date from the early centuries of the Iron Age, from 1000 B.C. onwards.

This later group of bronzes in particular recalls aspects of contemporary history which we have already briefly mentioned; and this helps to explain the actual character of the objects themselves. For this was the period which saw an almost continuous movement of Indo-European horsemen migrating from the north; and the contents of the graves in fact consist of 'nomads' gear'—the portable goods and chattels of wandering tribes, for which, as the nomads passed, the settled craftsmen in the towns and villages of Iran must have found a continual demand. Foremost among them are chariot- or harness-fittings; rein-rings, bits, and ornaments, as well as weapons and various types of talisman. The style of ornament is here both

235

194 Rein-ring; reminiscent of Sumerian art, but attributed to the first half of the second millennium B.C.

ingenious and elegant and the talent which produced it must clearly be attributed to an indigenous school of craftsmen, rather than to the transitory presence of migrant tribes. The style has in fact many characteristics which are essentially Iranian and which, in their perfected form, will presently be discussed in connexion with Achaemenian Persian art. Apart from this there is much that reflects the traditional contacts of this region with Mesopotamia.

Some of the earliest of these bronzes take the form of rein-rings, and one of them in particular may have helped to create the initial illusion that the bronzes might date from Sumerian times (*Ill. 194*).

236

195 A talisman; the old motif of the 'hero between beasts' is now formalized almost beyond recognition

196 Another talisman. This is free-standing and the bottle-shaped base gives it stability

In general appearance it closely resembles for instance the one from Ur illustrated in *Ill. 58*. It is surmounted by the figures of two men. One, dressed in a Sumerian 'kilt', is slaying a naked foe and both have eyes inlaid in the Sumerian manner. The belated use here in the second millennium of devices long superseded in Sumer itself is certainly strange. Another rein-ring has two ibexes confronting each other on either side of a sacred tree. Animals such as the 'hero between beasts' (Gilgamesh?) (*Ill. 195-7*), sphinxes, or griffins, are also very commonly found on bits and harness-rings. The former, which may be either linked or rigid, are also

237

197 Cheek-piece from Luristan. The Mesopotamian motif once more appears in an earlier and less stylized form

198 Bronze votive effigy from Payravand. Like much else in Iranian art of this period, the significance of this figure is unknown to us

fitted with heavy cheek-pieces and these are decorated with cut-out or pierced designs (*Ill. 200*). The character of the ornament is fairly constant; both here and on most other fittings such as staff-heads and 'standards' it consists of magic devices intended to protect the horses. But there are also human talismans (*Ill. 195–6*) —bronze emblems fitted into a bottle-shaped base; and here the repertory of animals is more varied and their stylized forms particularly attractive. Ibex, antelope, various felines, and even flamingoes make a range of subjects occasionally varied by the figure of a

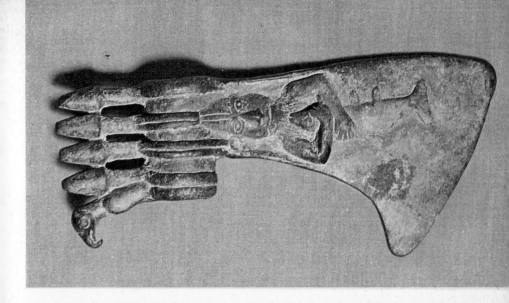

199 (*above*) Bronze axe-head from Luristan. Another funerary treasure whose symbolism cannot be interpreted

200 (*below*) Cheek-pieces with bit. The occupants of the Iranian graves were skilled horsemen

201 Detail of a gold cup from Hasanlu in Azerbaijan. Thought to be Manaean work and dated about 900 B.C. There is a whole range of mythological subjects of which we remain totally ignorant

fertility goddess with hands upon her breasts. There are also halberd- and axe-heads, some of the latter with spikes at the back (*Ill. 199*) being immediately reminiscent of that carried by the 'warrior' figure from the 'King's Gate' at Boghazköy. Among the Iron Age bronzes, a group of metal 'buckets' or *situlae* without handles fall into a rather separate category, since the *repoussé* designs are almost exclusively borrowed from Assyria (*Ill. 186*). The latest group of all, known as the 'Payravand Bronzes', are clearly votive figures representing some barbarous by-way of Iranian superstition (*Ill. 198*).

There is little if anything to suggest that the Persian dynasty which came to power in the sixth century B.C. found a ready-made mantle of Iranian cultural tradition in which to clothe itself. On the contrary, the Persians themselves, as nomads or semi-nomads having no more than an average appreciation of applied arts and craftsmanship on a small scale, must have sought in vain for any indigenous form of monumental art. This, at all events, was undoubtedly the situation with which Cyrus was faced when, after his defeat of Nabonidus, he found himself invested with the portentous title of 'King of Babylon', and became master of a great Empire. And the Achaemenian art which we today know and admire, owes its individuality to the synthesis of styles which, in these circumstances, he and his successors so intelligently created. A new element in its composition resulted from the first encounter of an Oriental people with the genius of Greek artists. By the time of Darius, in fact, Greek craftsmen in large numbers were undoubtedly employed at the Persian court. At the same time the basic form of expression continued to follow very closely the traditions of Mesopotamia. The successful evolution from these ingredients of an authentically imperial art must be credited partly to the contribution of a third and purely Iranian element by the Persians themselves. The native intelligence which enabled them to master its practice and to understand its potentialities is also much to be admired.

So we have today, in the Persian rock-sculptures, in the palaces or tombs of Persepolis and Susa, in the astonishing hoards of Persian jewellery which have from time to time been recovered from the ground, an assemblage of representative art-works of more than sufficient quantity to convey the magnitude of Achaemenian achievement. The first fact which they make abundantly clear is the preponderance of the 'third element' referred to in our previous paragraph—the hereditary aptitude for decorative design inherent in the Iranian mentality, which, when given full rein, eventually enabled these remarkable people to create both a style and an equipment of cardinal art-forms, excelling in some respects the foreign and traditional models from which they were adapted.

In this connexion Upham Pope, author of the most voluminous work on the subject, who is inclined to attribute most characteristics of Achaemenian art to Iranian heredity, traceable back to the ceramic artists of a remote prehistoric period, has offered the most eloquent appraisal of their quality. 'The predominance', he says, 'of the decorative interest, which may be accounted the outstanding and almost unfailing characteristic of Iranian art, provided a common foundation through all changes of fashion, from prehistoric to modern times. Corollary to this are the decorative ideals that were spontaneously sustained: clarity, precision, ordered arrangement, rhythmic design, the use of expressive silhouettes, and meticulous craftsmanship. Vitalizing these principles, which seem to have been a natural endowment in all the successive phases of Iranian culture, is an inexhaustible talent for invention, a faculty which seems to be self-generating for devising original, striking, and felicitous forms. Moreover, in practically all kinds of composition there is maintained an aristocratic reserve. Yet this is not just a negative restraint. There is an affirmative, even extravagant, love of elaboration and splendour

202 Darius giving audience, from the treasury at Persepolis. Xerxes, the heir-apparent, stands beside him. They are both on a larger scale than their attendants. The official being received is a Mede

203 Detail of the stairway to the 'Tripylon', Persepolis. Unlike the Assyrian reliefs which decorate the interior of palaces, these Persian sculptures embellish the external approaches to public buildings

that occasionally does exceed its proper bounds and would do so oftener were it not for a prevailing demand for elegance.'

The surviving monuments are for the most part sculptures in relief (free-standing statues do not seem to have been a concept acceptable to the Persians), sculptured architectural components, glazed-brick reliefs, bronze and gold jewellery. The best-known reliefs are from the great palace at Persepolis, a building whose construction and decoration passed through three stages corresponding to the reigns of Darius I, Xerxes, and Artaxerxes I. It stands on a raised terrace about 545 yards long by 330 wide, and is approached by a broad stairway, over whose shallow treads a horseman could comfortably ride. Above this, an enormous square gate-house led to the main courtyards and to the throne hall ('Hall of a Hundred Columns') started by Xerxes and finished by his son, behind which were the residential palaces and the harem. The relief-sculpture is concentrated almost exclusively along the staircase façades, giving decorative emphasis to the main approaches (Ill. 203). In this way they differ a good deal in function from the reliefs in Assyrian palaces, which adorn the interior wall-faces of assembly-halls and audience-chambers. This fact has been taken to explain a conspicuous disparity between the actual subjects respectively chosen for the Assyrian and Persian carvings. The former lend themselves above all to the narrative portrayal of actual events, which are sometimes even clarified by commentary inscriptions; and these the waiting courtiers would have had leisure to study at close quarters. In common, therefore, with sculptured scenes in Egyptian tombs, they developed a power of expression which required a considerable freedom of design. The Achaemenid reliefs on the other hand, which were intended to take their place as an integral part of an architectural design—a superficial enrichment emphasizing the shape of a façade—had less to fear from monotonous formality in the repetition of stylized figures. And indeed the reliefs at Persepolis do suffer from extreme monotony of subject. The audience scenes in particular, with their attendance of servants and processions of figures bringing tribute, are in reality even more repetitive than the usual selective photographs of detail would suggest.

244

204 Relief from Persepolis. The interest in folded drapery has been aroused by contact with Greek sculptors (see *Ill. 249*)

But a much more fundamental distinction between these Achaemenian sculptures and those of Assyria lies in a changed approach to the principles of relief-carving, which is clearly inspired by familiarity with Greek art. Assyrian reliefs remain basically two-dimensional pictures, in that the figures are merely raised above the background in a series of parallel horizontal planes. Any modelling that is introduced is subordinated to these, and on the whole engraved detail is preferred. By contrast, in the Persian reliefs, the figures stand out as protruding masses of three-dimensional forms. Occasionally even, anatomical modelling is suggested beneath the fabric of a garment and the plastic treatment of drapery is already beginning to be understood (*Ill. 204*). But their general

245

205 (*above*) Glazed-brick-relief of a griffin, from Susa. The colouring is brilliant, but the modelling does not show the precision of stone-carving

206 (*right*) Figures of warriors in glazed bri from Susa, members of the Persian ro guard. These panels may be compared wi the 'Ishtar Gate' at Babylon (*Ill. 190–1*)

effect is that of a 'metallic' finish—as though these craftsmen had originally been bronze-casters and built their detail in clay rather than carving it in stone.

Moreover, it should be borne in mind that the Persian reliefs, like many of their prototypes in Assyria, must originally have been bright with colour. Turquoise and lapis-lazuli blue, scarlet, green, purple, and yellow have all left traces on the stone, while metal ornaments showed remnants of gilding. At Susa panels of glazed bricks were used, but there was little departure here from the technique associated with this form of ornament in Babylon. Only a frieze of armed men is an innovation, together with another of lions, over which an Egyptian motif has intruded in the form of lotus ornament (*Ill. 206*).

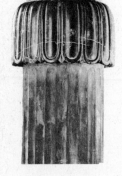

Double-bull capitals (*207, left*) from Persepolis and (*208, right*) from Susa. These sculptured imposts, which provide a wide bearing for the beam which they carried, are a peculiarly Persian device; but there is a hint of Greek architecture in the fluting and in the volutes of the Susa example

A most characteristic feature of Achaemenian architecture are its columns. (The throne-rooms and audience-halls, with their elementary square shapes and forests of ornamental pillars, may be reminiscent of the elaborate tent-pavilions in which Persian chieftains held court in tribal days.) The details and mouldings of Persian columns have a strong resemblance to Ionic prototypes, seen in the Greek cities of the Aegean coast, which now fell within the dominion of the Achaemenian Empire. But one feature was without precedent in contemporary architecture. This was the impost-block or capital,

209 Face of a bull-man from a capital at Persepolis; the nearest approach made by Persian sculptors to sculpture in the round. Here again is the almost 'metallic' finish, as though the figure had been modelled for casting rather than carved

surmounting the shaft-head, which was usually sculptured to resemble the foreparts of two kneeling animals (*Ill. 207–8*)—bulls, dragons, or occasionally bull-men (*Ill. 209*). This curious form of capital is said to be derived from the use of split saplings to support ceiling-beams in Persian houses. The strikingly decorative animal figures exemplify that satisfying collaboration between architect and sculptor which is so often evident in Persian composition.

These architectural sculptures are, as we have already said, the nearest approach to carving in the round ever made by artists in Achaemenian times. For actual statues, one must turn to metal-work. In this category, a few standing figures on a small scale have been preserved, of which perhaps the most distinguished is the solid silver figure of an elaborately dressed man, now in the British Museum (*Ill. 212*). But there is elsewhere no lack of evidence for the popularity and proficiency of Achaemenian metal-workers. Both ornamental vessels (*Ill. 210*) and jewellery appear in great variety among the subjects of the relief-carvings; while chance finds in Persia have brought to light proof of their superb craftsmanship in the most convincing forms. One conspicuous group, the so-called 'Oxus Treasure' (*Ill. 211, 213*) has enriched the British Museum; another from a tomb near Susa is in the Louvre, while a third, whose provenance can only be guessed, reached the market as recently as 1955 and is now divided between the Metropolitan and Teheran Museums (*Ill. 215*). There are rhytons (drinking-vessels), daggers, bracelets, necklaces, and small vessels in gold; while some of the most beautiful pieces of all are handles in animal-form from

→

211 Griffin rhyton; silver, from the 'Oxus Treasure'. The vessel obviously owes its shape to the drinking-horn. The creature is the same as that represented in glazed brick in *Ill. 205*.

212 Silver figure of a man, one of the few figures in the round dating from Achaemenian times

larger vessels of bronze. All of them show the remarkable Iranian talent for ornament, which we first observed in the 'Luristan Bronzes', now perfected through long practice and increasing familiarity with foreign technology. And everywhere one sees in the detail of these creations, the hallmark of Persian taste in the love and understanding of animals and the formalization of their shapes for decorative purposes (*Ill. 213*). Remembering the artists of Eighteenth Dynasty Egypt, one realizes that this was really no more than a single aspect of a wider natural inclination—an awareness of

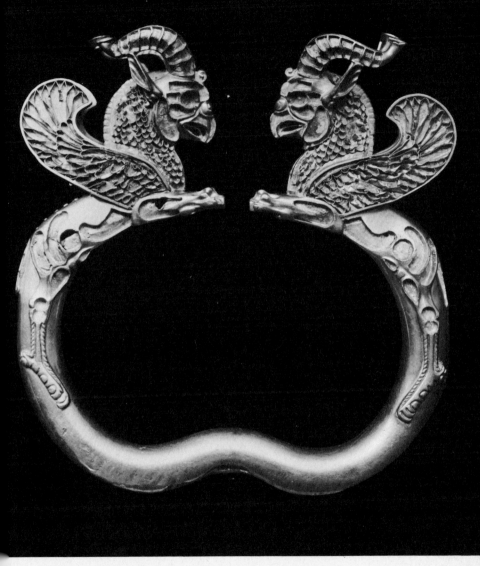

213 Gold bracelet from the 'Oxus Treasure'. This would originally have been encrusted with gems. The popular griffin figure appears again; the wings and oddly shaped ornament on the body resemble those in *Ill. 205*

214 Achaemenian cylinder-seals. *Top left:* Horse and camel; *top right:* Falcon and winged griffin; *bottom:* Hunting scene. Seal-carving now has much in common with relief-sculpture

natural beauty and a keenly responsive interest in the details of environment. It was reflected a little later in the love which the Persians developed for their gardens and in their original creation of 'paradises', enclosed sanctuaries where bird and animal life were protected.

And so at last, paradoxically we find ourselves reflecting on the creative sensibility of a people whose warlike ambition was in fact responsible for bringing the whole of our historical epoch to an

215 Gold dagger with lion- and ibex-heads. Part of a treasure (see *Ill. 210*) made, according to a tri-lingual inscription, specially for the Achaemenian kings

end. Their conquests, which extended from the frontiers of India to the Mediterranean, disrupted cultural life in the lands which they overran and the regional threads of artistic evolution were permanently severed.

In the sixth century B.C., then, this story ends. Yet today, in varying degrees, the lands of the Near East are still suffused with the aftermath of their creative past; and one need not resort to the sombre consolation of a museum in search of vanished splendours.

In the Nile Valley above all, from the temples of Thebes to the tombs of Sakkara, the spirit of Egyptian art calls to one and its beauty is still a tangible reality. As Leigh Hunt said of the river itself: 'It flows through old hushed Egypt and its sands, like some grave mighty thought threading a dream.'

In this brief study of Near Eastern art we have followed the evolution of man from his genesis to his first recorded achievements. Yet art, as distinct from his other creations, may be said like Aphrodite to have risen perfect from the waves of his creative thinking. No story need be sought of gradual development either in technique or inspiration; for it was born of individual intelligence and, itself like the sea, passed through storms of brilliance and calms of mediocrity. Our intention here has been merely to illuminate the crest of each wave in the phases of civilization which we have studied. In a work of this sort it would be wrong to seek a positive conclusion: for since man as a reflective being has spread the network of his thinking over the world known to him, art has been one of the main streams of his creative energy; not an accessory to his life, but as vital a part of it as the bloodstream itself. To express the full variety of his emotional experience, words have not sufficed; and as long as the springs of inspiration rise unimpeded in his mind, he will continue to interpret them in line, form, and colour.

An Outline of Architecture in the Near East

In the Near East, the earliest prehistoric farmers chose building materials according to their geographical environment. Settlers in the valleys and delta-lands of the great rivers either used reeds plastered with mud or built up slabs of clay to harden in the sun. In rocky country to the north of the Syrian desert, stones could be piled to make a wall and were sometimes roughly shaped for the purpose. Already during the Neolithic period before 5000 B.C., sun-dried bricks began to replace the adobe of primitive builders and walls of this material, with or without stone foundations, soon became the most characteristic feature of Near Eastern buildings (*Ill. 216*). Forms of wood- and reed-structure, once popular in the river-valleys, simultaneously disappeared, though their influence on the principles of brick-building continued to be conspicuous and

216 Farm-house at Hassuna

has been taken to explain the peculiar recessing of brick façades both in Egypt and Mesopotamia (*Ill. 217*). An exceptional survival was the bell-shaped façade of the standard reed-building in the South Mesopotamian marshes, which can still be seen today. Its intricate design provided the symbol for a temple in the pictographs of Sumerian times (*Ill. 23*).

The centuries immediately before 3000 B.C. in these countries saw the first conscious attempts at architectural design which culminated in the contrivance of really impressive public buildings. In Mesopotamia the mud-brick temples of the Al 'Ubaid period,

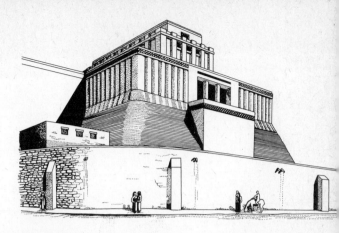

218 Temple at Eridu on stone-faced platform

with their recessed outer walls, were now set upon a high brick
platform (*Ill. 218*). Kiln-baked bricks were already used in small
quantities and wall-faces were decorated with mosaics composed of
terracotta cones whose ends were dipped in colour or sheathed in
copper (*Ill. 219*). A high sanctuary in the centre was lit by clerestory
windows and the gloom of the surrounding chambers brightened
by painted frescoes (*Ill. 221*). In Egypt brick *mastaba* tombs with
panelled façades foreshadowed the stone pyramids of dynastic times.

219 Reconstruction of mosaic decoration in the Pillared Hall at Warka (cf. *Ill. 25*)

220 (*right*) Reconstruction of the entrance
colonnade in *Ill. 222*

221 (*below*) Reconstruction of the altar and
frescoes of the temple at Tell 'Uqair

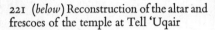

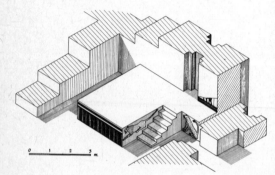

The character of Egyptian architecture in the Dynastic period
was subject to three primary influences. First, there were geological
circumstances which provided an abundance of building stone in
many varieties: limestone in the escarpments of the Nile Valley from
Cairo to Luxor, sandstone farther south and granite elsewhere as well
as alabaster, basalt, and porphyry. Next there was the climate—the
almost cloudless brilliance of the Egyptian skies—which made the
exclusion of heat a more important consideration than the admission
of light. And one sees lastly the effects of a social system which
made organized labour available in almost unlimited quantities.

An architectural style of remarkable subtlety and without
apparent antecedents appears fully fledged in the time of the Third
Dynasty (*Ill. 220, 222*). The 'Step Pyramid' and funerary buildings of
Zoser at Sakkara (*Ill. 223–5*) show not only the skilful adaptation of

222 Entrance colonnade to Zoser's Hall of Pillars, Sakkara

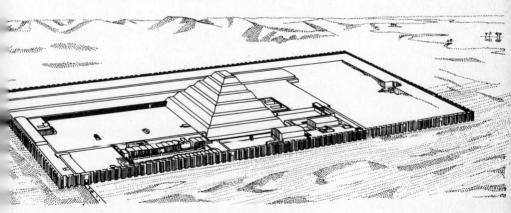

223 Reconstruction of Zoser's pyramid complex, Sakkara

224 Capital from Zoser's tomb area at Sakkara

mud-brick conventions to the art of building in stone, but also the confident handling of organic shapes—papyrus and other plant-forms (*Ill. 224*)—as structural ornament. Even the wooden ceiling-beams of earlier days, now transformed into stone, make an attractive ornamental device, while curved planes and delicate fluting seem at times to anticipate the Doric refinements of classical Greece (*Ill. 225*). But this phase seems to have been short-lived. Its delicate refinement is almost immediately superseded by the ponderous monumentality of the pyramid age. A cross-section through Zoser's tomb shows successive stages in the evolution of the pyramid from the old-fashioned brick *mastaba* by superimposing similar elements of diminishing size. The form of a 'staged tower' was thus created to express in the simplest form an elementary aspiration of earthbound humanity. By the time of the Fourth

225 Fluted columns of Zoser's temple, with the 'Step Pyramid' in the background

Dynasty this conception had acquired the austerity of an unequivocal geometric form (*Ill. 226*) whose internal arrangements and architectural dependencies were ordered and disposed with the logic of maturing religious conviction (*Ill. 227*). Meanwhile, for Zoser's finely jointed limestone the hard granite of Upper Egypt had been substituted in blocks of cyclopean proportions, and his fluted pilasters were replaced by huge monolithic columns, whose formal ornament retained little trace of the earlier, more elegant naturalism.

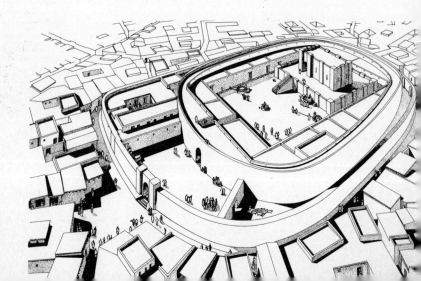

227 Reconstruction of the 'Great Pyramid' with funerary boat

Dynastic Sumerians during the early third millennium B.C. devoted their talents to designing temples rather than tombs. The mud-brick platform on which their primary shrine had already been raised (*Ill. 228*) was now heightened and elaborated, like the Egyptian pyramid, into a staged tower of the type known as a *ziggurat* (*Ill. 229*). These huge structures were faced with kiln-baked bricks, panelled and recessed to break the monotony of their colossal façades, strengthened with bitumen and reinforced with twisted reeds (*Ill. 230*). Such, for instance, was the *ziggurat* at Birs Nimrod (Babylon), which tradition associates with 'The Tower of Babel'. It usually stood within a walled *temenos* or enclosure, containing other temples variously dedicated. These as usual were of brick, with buttressed and recessed façades terminating in flat roofs. The basic plan consisted of a sanctuary and dependent chambers, but in the larger examples this unit could be multiplied by means of communicating courtyards (*Ill. 231*). Wall-ornaments,

229 Reconstruction of Ur Nammu's *ziggurat* at Ur

228 Reconstruction of the temple oval at Khafaje

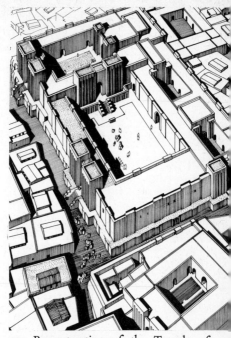

231 Reconstruction of the Temple of Ishtar Kititum at Ischali

232 Temple of Amon at Karnak, the 'Great Hall of Pillars'

233 Temple of Amon at Karnak, the 'South Hall', showing papyrus and lotus ornament

which are found only in such buildings dating from the early Sumerian dynasties, include square stone plaques sculptured in low relief, panels with mythical groups or animals' heads built up in bitumen and sheathed in bronze, and friezes with religious scenes inlaid in white limestone and rosettes or other ornaments carved from coloured stones and affixed to the ends of terracotta nails.

Among remains of the second millennium B.C. in Mesopotamia, palaces and other secular buildings are more in evidence. But they have little to distinguish them architecturally save a large rectangular throne-room, entered like the sanctuary of a temple through a wide doorway on its short axis from an open court. The first signs of ornament in these buildings occur in the Kassite period about 1500 B.C., when painted frescoes appear at the base of internal walls, foreshadowing the sculptured reliefs of Assyrian times. Private dwellings at this time, like the more pretentious buildings, have rooms facing on to and obtaining light from a central court-yard in the Oriental manner (*Ill. 234*).

The architecture of the second millennium B.C. in Egypt offers a most striking contrast to the pedestrian austerity of Mesopotamian design. The monumental compositions in stone achieved at this time by the inhabitants of the Nile Valley have become for succeeding generations such a commonplace item of hereditary experience, that the creative miracle by which they were conceived and perfected tends today to be hardly appreciated. It is easy to forget that never before in human history had the religious and political convictions of a great nation been expressed in a material form so convincing that it could be universally apprehended and so permanent as to be almost ineffaceable. One substantial chapter in the history of its evolution indeed happens to be poorly documented. From the so-called Middle Kingdom hardly a single monument survived the subsequent disturbances which led to the Hyksos conquest. Fortunately, however, the maturity and perfection of Egyptian style is more than amply illustrated by the buildings whose remains the New Kingdom has bequeathed to posterity.

This Egyptian style, then, is exclusively adapted to stone architecture. Of brick-buildings in Mesopotamia, which we have

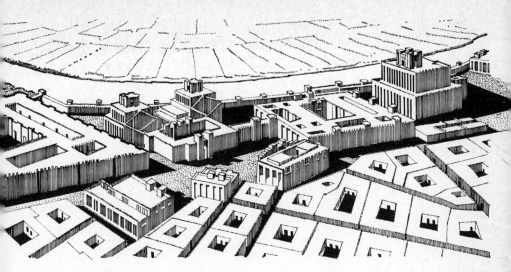

234 Reconstruction of the city of Assur

mentioned, one peculiarity is the absence of columns and the consequent roofing difficulties apparent in the shapes of the chambers. For roofing in Egypt stone was used, as it was for almost every other purpose, and this resulted in a structural system which is sometimes described as 'columnar and trabeate' (*Ill. 236*). A forest of columns divides the enclosed chambers into units, small enough to be spanned by a network of stone lintels with flat slabs sealing the spaces between. The difficulty in these circumstances of obtaining sufficient light led to the invention of the so-called 'hypostyle hall'. In this, two ranges of columns on the central axis were given increased height, in order to obtain a vertical clerestory between them and their neighbours, in which stone-grilled windows could be inserted. In such buildings two main types of columns were in general use, both having sculptural forms adapted from plant motifs (*Ill. 233*). One, with a shaft curving inwards at the base, had a capital in the form of a lotus or papyrus bud. The other, with a simple tapered shaft, was crowned with the inverted bell shape of a papyrus flower. The latter was used mainly for the central hypostyle pillars and in other conspicuous positions. Characteristic also were the portals formed from pairs of pylons—towers with

269

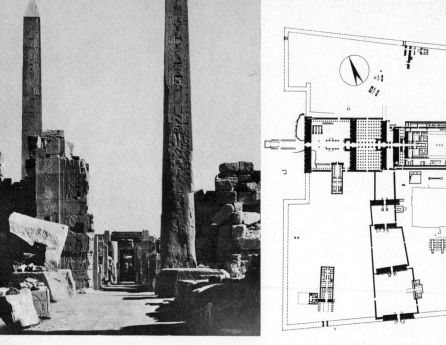

235 Temple of Amon at Karnak, showing
Queen Hatshepsut's obelisk

236 Plan of the temple of Amon
at Karnak

sloped faces, chased vertically to receive ornamental masts perhaps
carrying banners. A succession of these portals was used to emphasize the single cardinal axis, along which the whole disposal of the
building was arranged, from the avenue of sculptured figures at the
approach, through outer court and hypostyle hall, to the dark
labyrinth of cult-chambers behind, to which only priests and
royalty had access (*Ill. 236*). In the public chambers and halls,
sculptured reliefs and carved hieroglyphic inscriptions were
ubiquitous, as may be gathered from a glance at the illustrations,
and a very general use was made of colour.

These, then, were features common to most of the great temples
at Luxor and Thebes. But others were added at various times, including the obelisks, for which a special courtyard was sometimes
provided (*Ill. 235*), the 'Osiris pillars' sometimes found in mortuary

237 Queen Hatshepsut's temple at Deir-el-Bahri

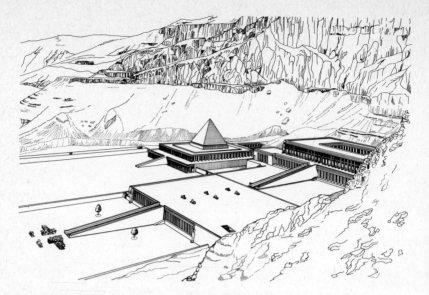

238 Reconstruction of Queen Hatshepsut's temple at Deir-el-Bahri with the Eleventh Dynasty temple of Menthu-hetep II behind

temples, which could be considered the forerunners of the Greek caryatids, and the so-called 'Hathor-head capitals', with the sculptured face of the goddess surmounted by a small shrine. There were temples, like the beautiful terraced building erected by Queen Hatshepsut at Deir-el-Bahri (*Ill. 237–8*), which diverge from the conventional plan in order to adapt themselves to a special setting— in this case a magnificent site at the base of the Theban cliffs (*Ill. 238*). There were also funerary temples, differently planned, one of them even incorporating a small pyramid. And finally there were the rock-cut temples like that of Ramesses II at Abu Simbel to which we have referred elsewhere (see *Ill. 153*).

With this great wealth of stone buildings to study, the humbler mud-brick structures—administrative dependencies of temples and ordinary dwelling-houses—have received less attention from archaeologists. But there are good examples of the former surrounding the temple of Ramesses II at Thebes (*Ill. 239*): and Akhenaten's short-lived capital at Tell-el-Amarnah has revealed the most elegant mud-brick palaces and mansions, with wood-pillared rooms, frescoed walls, formal gardens, and ornamental pavilions (*Ill. 240*).

239 Funerary temple of Ramesses II, Thebes

Before the end of the second millennium B.C. is reached historically, other countries of the Near East are found to be competing with Egypt and Mesopotamia in developing an architectural style of their own. In Anatolia in particular, the Hittites built huge stone temples of a type best illustrated by the ruins of their capital city, Hattusas (now called Boghazköy) (*Ill. 241*). This city had a high citadel and a two-mile circuit of defensive walls which in themselves are a striking architectural accomplishment (*Ill. 242*). Placed upon a high rampart of earth, the huge stones of their substructure were finely jointed but not laid in regular courses, and the

240 Reconstruction of a house at Tell-el-Amarnah

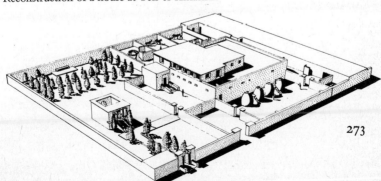

273

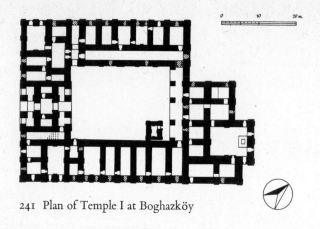

241 Plan of Temple I at Boghazköy

superstructure was of mud-brick. At intervals there were gateways with corbelled arches between towers, and the openings themselves were flanked by sculptured portal-figures, one pair, in the form of sphinxes, anticipating by five hundred years the winged bulls and lions which later became such a common feature of Assyrian palaces. But the normal form of construction throughout Anatolia, which dated from the earliest centuries of the Bronze Age, continued to be that which in Europe today is known as 'half-timber'—panels of brickwork set in a framework of wooden beams. This gives to a building the elasticity which is desirable even today in a land of frequent earthquakes.

242 Reconstruction of the city-walls at Boghazköy

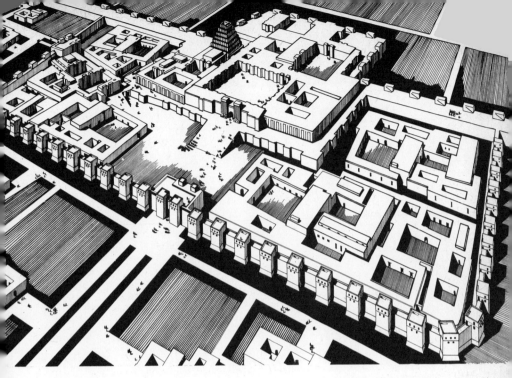

243 Reconstruction of part of the citadel at Khorsabad

The rise of Assyria to imperial power in the early centuries of the first millennium B.C. gave new vitality to Mesopotamian architecture. The huge mud-brick palaces brought to light by early European archaeologists symbolize the ostentatious grandeur of the Assyrian kings. Like the temples of earlier days, they too were now usually built on a high brick platform, their gates flanked by colossal portal-sculptures and their chambers decorated with pictorial reliefs carved on stone slabs. These and other ornamental features have been referred to elsewhere (pages 193 ff.), while the general planning and appearance of such building complexes can best be understood from the admirable architectural reconstructions made by more recent excavators (*Ill. 243*). During the Late Assyrian period, vassal States in North Syria and Taurus, inhabited by remnants of the Hittites, devised some architectural features peculiar to themselves (*Ill. 244*). One of these was a broad portico, supported by wooden

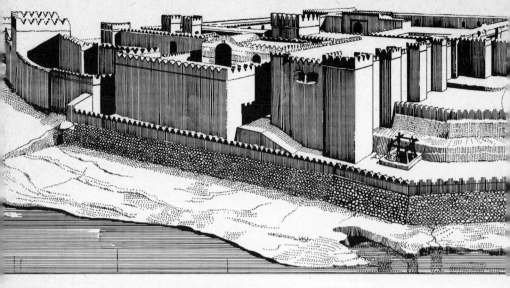

244 Reconstruction of Sinjerli

columns (*Ill. 245*), which stood upon sculptured bases, strikingly contrived from paired animal figures. Sculptured capitals also introduced some new ornamental motifs.

The Babylonian renaissance, following the fall of Assyria in 612 B.C. brought many new buildings to South Mesopotamia, but their style remained strictly traditional. In Nebuchadnezzar's Babylon almost the only novelty was the brilliant colour of the glazed bricks with which the 'Procession Street' and buildings of the inner city were so copiously adorned, and the reliefs which enriched their surface with a delicate pattern of shadows. But in Persia,

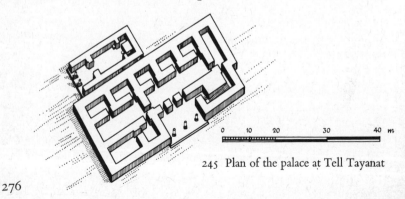

245 Plan of the palace at Tell Tayanat

246 Achaemenian royal tomb at Naqsh-i-Rustam

when the contemporary Achaemenian dynasty began to build on a
large scale, the Iranian genius for design gave a strong individuality
to the synthesis of existing styles (*Ill. 246*). This was not however
accompanied by any aptitude for general planning or the grouping
of buildings. On the great rock-cut terrace at Persepolis, the various
palaces (*Ill. 247*) and porticoes, with the wide sculptured stairways
which approach them, are disposed in an unconsidered relationship
that seems almost haphazard, and recalls the grouping of tent-
pavilions in the centre of a nomad encampment. The famous 'Hall

277

of a Hundred Columns' (*Ill. 248*) itself is no more than a monotonous forest of pillars, squarely enclosed in blank walls. The
Iranian accomplishment in fact lies mainly in the sculptured reliefs
with which these architects, preferring to ornament the external
approaches to their buildings rather than the internal wall-faces,
enlivened their propylae and porticoes (*Ill. 249*) and in the glazed-
brick friezes and the elaborately decorative columns with their
twin-bull capitals.

249 Relief from the 'Hall of a Hundred Columns' (cf. *Ill. 204*)

248 Reconstruction of portico leading to the 'Hall of a Hundred Columns' (cf. *Ill. 207*)

	EGYPT	MESOPOTAMIA	ANATOLIA	SYRIA-PALESTINE	IRAN	
	CHALCOLITHIC PHASES					
BC 4500						
4000	Fayum 'A' Tasian Badarian Amratian Gerzean (All Pre- Dynastic)	Hassuna Samarra Tell Halaf Al 'Ubaid Uruk		CONTEMPORARY CHALCOLITHIC PHASES AT MANY SITES		
3500		PROTOLITERATE				
3000	PROTO- DYNASTIC AND OLD KINGDOM	EARLY DYNASTIC PHASES I, II AND III	FIRST EARLY BRONZE AGE (TROY I) SECOND EARLY BRONZE AGE (TROY II)	FIRST TO FOURTH EARLY BRONZE AGE		2600 2400
2500	FIRST INTER- MEDIATE PERIOD	AKKAD LAGASH	ALACA TOMBS THIRD EARLY BRONZE AGE		GUTI	2300 2134
2000	MIDDLE KINGDOM	UR III / ISIN- LARSA	(TROY III AND IV) MIDDLE BRONZE AGE (KULTEPE)	MIDDLE BRONZE AGE		1900
	SECOND INTER- MEDIATE PERIOD	FIRST DYNASTY OF BABYLON	HITTITE (OLD KINGDOM)		ELAMITE	1778
1500	NEW KINGDOM	KASSITES (EARLY ASSYRIAN)	HITTITE (EMPIRE)	FOREIGN DOMINATION TO LATE BRONZE AGE	KINGDOM	1576 1450
1000	LATE PERIOD	ASSYRIAN	URARTU / PHRYGIAN / NEO- HITTITE	IRON AGE		1085
500		NEO-BABYLONIAN	LYDIAN		MEDES ACHAEMENIAN SUPREMACY	612 525
	PERIOD OF PERSIAN DOMINATION					

250 Outline chronology of the ancient Near East. The right-hand column indicates fixed historical dates

Bibliography

List of Illustrations

Index

Bibliography

It would clearly be impracticable in a work of this size to provide a complete or even adequate bibliography of so vast a subject. We must be content to put forward the following list of appropriate or easily available works covering between them almost every subject illustrated, since their texts can amplify our own commentary and their combined bibliographies give direction for further reading.

AKURGAL, E. *Phrygische Kunst* 1955

ALDRED, C. *Development of Ancient Egyptian Art* ('Chapters in Art' Series) 1952

BARNETT, R. D. *Catalogue of the Nimrûd Ivories in the British Museum* 1957

BARNETT, R. D. *Assyrian Palace Reliefs* [1960]

BOSSERT, H. TH. *Altanatolien* 1942

BOSSERT, H. TH. *Altsyrien* 1951

COSTA, A. and LOCKHART, L. *Persia* 1957

DAVIES, N. DE G. *Rock Tombs of El Amarna VI* (Egypt Exploration Society) 1908

DAVIES, NINA M. *Picture Writing in Ancient Egypt* 1959

DAVIES, NINA M. and GARDINER, A. H. *Ancient Egyptian Paintings* 1936

DRIOTON, ÉTIENNE *Art Egyptien* 1950

FRANKFORT, H. *Cylinder Seals* 1939

FRANKFORT, H. *Birth of Civilization in the Near East* 1951

FRANKFORT, H. *Art and Architecture of the Ancient Orient* (Pelican History of Art) 1954

FRANKFORT, H. and others *Mural Paintings of El-'Amarneh* (Egypt Exploration Society) 1929

FRANKFORT, H. A. G. *Arrest and Movement* 1951

GADD, C. J. *Stones of Assyria* 1936

GHIRSHMANN, R. *Iran* (Penguin Books) 1954

GÖTZE, A. *Kulturgeschichte des Alten Orients* 1957

HALL, H. R. *Babylonian and Assyrian Sculptures in the British Museum* 1928

HOLTZMEISTER, C. and G. *Bilder aus Anatolien* 1955

KOŞAY, H. Z. *Les Fouilles d'Alaça Hüyük* (Türk Tarih Kurumu) 1951

LANGE, K. and HIRMER, MAX *Egypt: Architecture, Sculpture and Painting in Three Thousand Years* (2nd ed.) 1957

LLOYD, SETON *Early Anatolia* (Penguin Books) 1956

MEKHITARIAN, A. *Egyptian Painting* 1954

NAUMANN, R. *Architektur Kleinasiens* 1953

ÖZGÜÇ, N. and T. *Kültepe*, 1950, –53, –60 (Türk Tarih Kurumu)

PARROT, ANDRÉ *Mari* 1953

PARROT, ANDRÉ *Sumer* (The Arts of Mankind) 1960

PATERSON, A. *Assyrian Sculptures in the Palace of Sennacherib* 1915

RIEMSCHNEIDER, M. *Die Welt der Hethiter* (Grosse Kulturen der Frühzeit) 3rd ed. 1954

RUNDLE CLARK, R. T. *Myth and Symbol in Ancient Egypt* 1959

SCHÄFER, H. and ANDRAE, W. *Die Kunst des Alten Orients* 1925

STEVENSON SMITH, W. *The Art and Architecture of Ancient Egypt* (Pelican History of Art) 1958

UPHAM POPE, A. *A Survey of Persian Art* 1938

VANDIER, J. and NAGUIB, M. *Egypt: Paintings from Tombs and Temples* (UNESCO World Art Series) 1956

VIEYRA, M. *Hittite Art* ('Chapters in Art' Series) 1955

VON DER OSTEN, H. H. *Die Welt der Perser* (Grosse Kulturen der Frühzeit) 2nd ed. 1956

VON OPPENHEIM, M. *Tell Halaf* 1930

WALLIS BUDGE, E. A. *Assyrian Sculptures in the British Museum* 1914

WOOLLEY, C. L. *Development of Sumerian Art* 1935

List of Illustrations

The author and publishers are grateful to the many official bodies, institutions, and individuals mentioned below for their assistance in supplying original illustration material.

284

25 Painted pots from Tell Asmar, Jemdet Nasr period. Department of Antiquities, Ashmolean Museum, Oxford. Photo: Eileen Tweedy.

26 Statuette of Pepy I, from Sakkara. Brooklyn Museum. Photo: Charles Uht.

27 Pair-statue of Mykerinus and his Queen, from Giza. Boston Museum of Fine Arts. Photo: Boston Museum.

28 Rahotep and Nofret, from Meidum. Cairo Museum. Photo: Max Hirmer.

29 Statue of the vizier Herniunu from Giza. Pelizaeus Museum, Hildesheim. Photo: Wehmeyer.

30 Head of Prince Ankh-kaf, from Giza. Boston Museum of Fine Arts. Photo: Boston Museum.

31 'Reserve head' of daughter-in-law of Cheops. Boston Museum of Fine Arts. Photo: Boston Museum.

32 Granite head, from Sakkara. Cairo Museum. Photo: Max Hirmer.

33 Limestone head of Mykerinus, from Giza. Boston Museum of Fine Arts. Photo: Boston Museum.

34 King Kephren, from Giza. Cairo Museum. Photo: Max Hirmer.

35 Statue (restored) of King Kha-Sekhem, from Hierakonopolis. Ashmolean Museum, Oxford. Photo: Department of Antiquities, Ashmolean Museum.

36 Ivory label from a pair of sandals, from Abydos. British Museum. Photo: Courtesy Trustees of the British Museum.

37 Relief from the tomb of Ti, Sakkara. Photo: Max Hirmer.

38 Statue of King Zoser, from Sakkara. Cairo Museum. Photo: Max Hirmer.

39 Wooden panel from the tomb of Hesira, Sakkara. Cairo Museum. Photo: Max Hirmer.

40 Reliefs from the tomb of Mereruka, Sakkara. After the copy by the Oriental Institute, University of Chicago.

41 Relief of the god Geb, from the Zoser shrine, Heliopolis. Museo Egizio, Turin. Photo: Courtesy Superintendenza alle Antichità (Egittologia).

42 Relief of King Zoser from a door panel at Sakkara. Photo: Max Hirmer.

43 Relief from the tomb of Ptah-hotep, Sakkara. After: W. Wreszinski, *Atlas zur Altägyptischen Kulturgeschichte*, 1923–38, Taf. 2.

44 Cylinder-seal from Ur, Early Dynastic II. British Museum. Photo: Courtesy Trustees of the British Museum.

45 Copper relief of Im-dugud from Al 'Ubaid. British Museum. Photo: Courtesy Trustees of the British Museum.

46 The Ur 'Standard'; War panel. British Museum. Photo: John R. Freeman.

47 The Ur 'Standard'; Peace panel. British Museum. Photo: Courtesy Trustees of the British Museum.

48 Relief showing a feast, from Khafaje, with inserted fragment from Ur. Khafaje relief: Iraq Museum, Baghdad; Ur fragment: University Museum, Philadelphia. Photo: Oriental Institute, University of Chicago.

49 Stela of Urnanshe, from Telloh. Louvre. Photo: Archives Photographiques.

50 Eannatum's stela, from Telloh (Lagash). Obverse and reverse of a fragment. Louvre. Photo: Archives Photographiques.

51 Carved steatite vase, from Khafaje. British Museum. Photo: John R. Freeman.

52 Gold bull's head on a lyre, from Ur. University Museum, Philadelphia. Photo: University Museum.

53 Golden helmet of Mes-kalam-shar, from Ur. Iraq Museum, Baghdad. Photo: Courtesy Directorate General of Antiquities, Iraq.

54 Head-dress of a woman from Ur on a model. Iraq Museum, Baghdad. Photo: Courtesy Directorate General of Antiquities, Iraq.

55 Gold fluted vase, from Ur. University Museum, Philadelphia. Photo: University Museum.

56 Gold dagger, from Ur. Iraq Museum, Baghdad. Photo: Courtesy Directorate General of Antiquities, Iraq.

57 'Ram caught in the thicket', from Ur. British Museum. Photo: John R. Freeman.

58 Ornamental rein-ring, from Ur. British Museum. Photo: Courtesy Trustees of the British Museum.

59 Cylinder-seal, 'Brocade' style, Early Dynastic I. British Museum. Photo: Oriental Institute, University of Chicago.

60 Cylinder-seal, Early Dynastic II. Iraq Museum, Baghdad. Photo: Courtesy Directorate General of Antiquities, Iraq.

61 Cylinder-seal, Early Dynastic III. British Museum. Photo: Courtesy Trustees of the British Museum.

62 Statuette of a priest, from Khafaje. University Museum, Philadelphia. Photo: Oriental Institute, University of Chicago.

63 The god Abu (?), 'worshipper' and female statue from Tell Asmar. Iraq Museum, Baghdad. Photo: Oriental Institute, University of Chicago.

64 'Worshipper' statue, head and shoulders, from Tell Asmar. Iraq Museum, Baghdad. Photo: Oriental Institute, University of Chicago.

65 Female head, from Tell Agrab. Iraq Museum, Baghdad. Photo: Oriental Institute, University of Chicago.

66 Group of stone mace-heads, from Tell Agrab. Iraq Museum, Baghdad. Photo: Oriental Institute, University of Chicago.

67 Steward Ebih-il, from Mari. Louvre. Photo: Courtesy Editions Ides et Calendes, Neuchâtel.

68 Copper statue, from Khafaje. Oriental Institute, University of Chicago. Photo: Oriental Institute.

69 Model chariot, from Tell Agrab. Iraq Museum, Baghdad. Photo: Oriental Institute, University of Chicago.

70 Life-sized bronze head of an Akkadian king from Nineveh. Iraq Museum, Baghdad. Photo: Courtesy of Directorate General of Antiquities, Iraq.

71 Stela of Naramsin, from Susa. Louvre. Photo: Archives Photographiques.

72 Diorite statue of Gudea of Lagash (Telloh), from Lagash. British Museum. Photo: Courtesy Trustees of the British Museum.

73 Another head of Gudea, from Lagash. Boston Museum of Fine Arts. Photo: Boston Museum.

74 Flagon and chalice of gold, disk and brooch, from Alaça Hüyük. Ankara Museum. Photo: Josephine Powell.

75 Stag-finial, from Alaça Hüyük. Ankara Museum. Photo: Josephine Powell.

76 Jewellery from 'Priam's Treasure', Troy. Archaeological Museum, Istanbul. Photo: Josephine Powell.

77 Jewellery from the royal tombs, Alaça Hüyük. Ankara Museum. Photo: Josephine Powell.

78 Head of Amenemhet III in basalt. Metropolitan Museum of Art, New York. Photo: Metropolitan Museum.

79 Head of Senusret III in red quartzite. Provenance unknown. Metropolitan Museum of Art, New York. Photo: Metropolitan Museum.

80 Statue of King Hor, from Dahshur. Cairo Museum. Photo: Max Hirmer.

81 Head of the Lady Sennuy, from Kerma, Sudan. Boston Museum of Fine Arts. Photo: Boston Museum.

82 Statue of Senusret-Senebef-Ni. Provenance unknown. Brooklyn Museum. Photo: Charles Uht.

83 Statue of Ameny. Provenance unknown. British Museum. Photo: Courtesy Trustees of the British Museum.

84 Paintings from the tomb of Knum-Hetep (copies). Two sections After: C. R. Lepsius, *Denkmäler aus Ägypten und Äthiopen*, 1849–1859, vol. 2, Taf. 133.

85 Head of woman with separate wig, from Lisht. Cairo Museum. Photo: George W. Allen.

86 Coffin of Knum-Hetep, from Deir Rifa, near Asyut. Royal Scottish Museum, Edinburgh. Photo: Royal Scottish Museum.

87 Funerary statue of Senusret I, from Lisht. Cairo Museum. After: H. G. Evers, *Staat aus dem Stein*, 1929, Taf. 97 b.

88 Senusret I and the god Ptah, from Karnak. Cairo Museum. Photo: Max Hirmer.

89 Model fishing-boat from the tomb of Meket-re. Deir-el-Bahri. Metropolitan Museum of Art, New York. Photo: Courtesy Metropolitan Museum of Art.

90 Two reliefs at Meir. Photo: Courtesy Egypt Exploration Society.

91 Hippopotamus, blue faience. Provenance unknown. Brooklyn Museum, loan from Mrs Bradley Martin. Photo: Brooklyn Museum.

92 Stela of Hammurabi, from Susa. Louvre. Photo: Archives Photographiques.

93 Head of a king, possibly Hammurabi, from Susa. Louvre. Photo: Archives Photographiques.

94 Statuette of the goddess Ningal, from Ur. University Museum, Philadelphia. Photo: University Museum.

95 Green stone bowl, with ibex, from Ischali. Oriental Institute, University of Chicago. Photo: Oriental Institute.

96 Fragment of wall-painting, from Mari. Louvre. Photo: Eileen Tweedy.

97 (*left*) Statue of Ishtup-Ilum, from Mari. Aleppo Museum. Photo: Courtesy André Parrot.

(*right*) Statue of Puzur-Ishtar, from Mari. Head: Ehemals Staatliches Museum, Berlin. Body: Archaeological Museum, Istanbul. Photo: Bildarchiv-Foto-Marburg and Archaeological Museum, Istanbul.

98 Offering-bearer, from Mari. Aleppo Museum. Photo: Courtesy Editions Ides et Calendes, Neuchâtel.

99 Two terracotta lions, from Harmal. Iraq Museum, Baghdad. Photo: Courtesy Directorate General of Antiquities, Iraq.

100 Bitch with puppies, terracotta plaque, from Khafaje. Oriental Institute, University of Chicago. Photo: Oriental Institute.

101 Warrior or god destroying a fiery cyclops, terracotta plaque, from Khafaje. Oriental Institute, University of Chicago. Photo: Oriental Institute.

102 Cylinder-seal, time of Hammurabi. Oriental Institute, University of Chicago. Photo: Oriental Institute.

103 Limestone head, Kassite period, from Dur Kurigalzu. Iraq Museum, Baghdad. Photo: Courtesy Directorate General of Antiquities, Iraq.

104 Façade ornament of Kassite temple, from Warka. Iraq Museum, Baghdad. Photo: Courtesy Directorate General of Antiquities, Iraq.

105 Terracotta head of a lioness, from Dur Kurigalzu. Iraq Museum, Baghdad. Photo: Courtesy Directorate General of Antiquities, Iraq.

106 Boar's head in faience, from Nuzi. Iraq Museum, Baghdad. Photo: Courtesy Directorate General of Antiquities, Iraq.

107 Mitannian painted pottery, from Atchana. Drawn by Diana Holmes after Woolley.

108 Mitannian cylinder-seal. Staatliche Museen, Berlin. Photo: Staatliche Museen.

109 Mitannian cylinder-seal. British Museum. Photo: Courtesy Trustees of the British Museum.

110 Mitannian cylinder-seal. British Museum. Photo: Courtesy Trustees of the British Museum.

111 Painted clay dog, from Kültepe. Ankara Museum. Photo: Josephine Powell.

112 Ivory winged griffin, from Megiddo. Oriental Institute, University of Chicago. Photo: Oriental Institute.

113 Line of running warriors, Yazilikaya. Photo: Josephine Powell.

114 A young king embraced by protecting god, Yazilikaya. Photo: Josephine Powell.

115 Head of Yarimlin of Alalakh. Antioch Museum. Photo: Courtesy the late Sir Leonard Woolley.

116 Ivory lid of box, from Minet-el-Beida. Louvre. Photo: M. Chuzeville.

117 Gold bowl, from Ras Shamra. Louvre. Photo: M. Chuzeville.

118 Painting from the tomb of the butler Wah, Thebes (copy by Nina M. Davies). Photo: Courtesy Oriental Institute, University of Chicago.

119 Relief from the tomb of Queen Hatshepsut, Deir-el-Bahri (Thebes). From a cast in the Royal Scottish Museum, Edinburgh. Photo: Tom Scott, Edinburgh.

120 Relief from the tomb of Queen Hatshepsut, Deir-el-Bahri (Thebes). Photo: Max Hirmer.

121 Painting from the tomb of Menna, Thebes. Photo: Max Hirmer.

122 Painting from the tomb of Neb-Amon, Thebes; unlocated. British Museum. Photo: Courtesy Trustees of the British Museum.

123 Painting from the tomb of Neb-Amon, Thebes; unlocated. British Museum. Photo: Eileen Tweedy.

124 Statuette of Negro girl, probably from the unlocated tomb of Mery-ptah, Thebes. Oriental Museum, University of Durham. Photo: University of Durham.

125 Painting from the tomb of Sen-Mut, Thebes (copy by Nina M. Davies). Photo: Courtesy Oriental Institute, University of Chicago.

126 Painting from the tomb of Neb-Amon, Thebes; unlocated. British Museum. Photo: Eileen Tweedy.

127 Statue of Queen Hatshepsut, from Deir-el-Bahri (Thebes). Metropolitan Museum of Art, New York. Photo: Metropolitan Museum.

128 Statue of Tuthmosis III, from the temple of Montu, Medamud. Metropolitan Museum of Art, New York. Photo: Metropolitan Museum.

129 Painting from the tomb of Horem-heb, Thebes (copy by Nina M. Davies). Photo: Courtesy Oriental Institute, University of Chicago.

130 Painting from the tomb of Rekh-mi-re at Thebes (copy by Nina M. Davies). Photo: Courtesy Metropolitan Museum of Art, New York.

131 Ivory figure of a gazelle, from Thebes. Metropolitan Museum of Art, New York. Photo: Metropolitan Museum.

132 Ivory statuette of a young girl, probably from Thebes. Brooklyn Museum. Photo: Brooklyn Museum.

133 Painting from the tomb of Rekh-mi-re, Thebes (copy by Nina M. Davies). Photo: Courtesy Metropolitan Museum of Art, New York.

134 Painting from the tomb of User-het, Thebes. Photo: Max Hirmer.

135 Painting from the tomb of Neb-Amon and Ipuki, Thebes. Photo: George W. Allen.

136 (a) Mycenaean fresco, Mycenae, (b) Egyptian Nineteenth Dynasty fresco, Abydos. Drawn by Diana Holmes after Frankfort.

137 Painting from the tomb of Horem-heb, Thebes (copy by Nina M. Davies). Photo: Courtesy Oriental Institute, University of Chicago.

138 Painting from the tomb of Rekh-mi-re, Thebes (copy by Nina M. Davies). Photo: Courtesy Metropolitan Museum of Art, New York.

139 Relief from the temple of Amon, Karnak. Photo: Max Hirmer.

140 'Caryatid' statue of Akhenaten, from Karnak. Cairo Museum. Photo: Max Hirmer.

141 Painting from the tomb of Nakht, Thebes. Photo: Max Hirmer.

142 Sculptor's relief model of Akhenaten and Nofretiti, from Tell-el-Amarnah. Brooklyn Museum. Photo: Brooklyn Museum.

143 Relief from the tomb of Ramose, Thebes. Photo: Max Hirmer.

144 Portrait-bust of Queen Nofretiti, from Tell-el-Amarnah. Staatliche Museen, Berlin. Photo: Max Hirmer.

145 Painting from the 'North Palace' of Tell-el-Amarnah (copy by Nina M. Davies). Photo: Courtesy Egypt Exploration Society.

146 Relief of Akhenaten and his family, from Tell-el-Amarnah. Staatliche Museen, Berlin. Photo: Walter Steinkopf.

147 Unfinished portrait-bust of Queen Nofretiti, from Tell-el-Amarnah. Cairo Museum. Photo: Max Hirmer.

148 Tutelary goddesses from the tomb of Tut-ankh-amon, Thebes. Cairo Museum. Photo: Courtesy Griffith Institute, Ashmolean Museum, Oxford.

149 Golden throne from the tomb of Tut-ankh-amon, Thebes. Cairo Museum. Photo: Max Hirmer.

150 Relief from the tomb of User-het, Thebes. Photo: Kurt Lange.

151 Relief of Sethos I as Osiris, Abydos. Photo: Max Hirmer.

152 Relief of the goddess Isis, Abydos. Photo: Max Hirmer.

153 Colossi of Ramesses II, Abu Simbel. Photo: Courtesy Director Général, Service des Antiquités, Cairo.

154 Middle Assyrian cylinder-seal. Pierpont Morgan Library, New York. Photo: Courtesy Trustees of the Pierpont Morgan Library.

155 Assyrian amber statuette of an unidentified king. Boston Museum of Fine Arts. Photo: Boston Museum.

156 Gateway to the palace at Khorsabad. Photo: Oriental Institute, University of Chicago.

157 Relief from the palace of Assurnasirpal, Nimrud. British Museum. Photo: Werner Forman.

158 Relief from the palace of Assurnasirpal, Nimrud. British Museum. Photo: Werner Forman.

159 Sargon II's citadel at Khorsabad. Reconstruction by G. Loud. Photo: Courtesy Oriental Institute, University of Chicago.

160 Relief from the palace of Sennacherib, Nineveh. British Museum. Photo: Courtesy Trustees of the British Museum.

161 Bronze relief from the 'Balawat Gates'. British Museum. Photo: Werner Forman.

162 Relief from the palace of Assurnasirpal, Nimrud. British Museum. Photo: Werner Forman.

163 Relief from the palace at Khorsabad. British Museum. Photo: Courtesy Trustees of the British Museum.

164 Relief from the palace of Assurbanipal, Nineveh. British Museum. Photo: Werner Forman.

165 Relief from the palace of Sennacherib, Nineveh. British Museum. Photo: Werner Forman.

166 Relief from the palace of Assurbanipal, Nineveh. British Museum. Photo: Courtesy Trustees of the British Museum.

167 Relief from the palace of Assurbanipal, Nineveh. British Museum. Photo: Courtesy Trustees of the British Museum.

168 Relief from the palace of Assurbanipal, Nineveh. British Museum. Photo: Werner Forman.

169 Relief from the palace of Assurbanipal, Nineveh. British Museum. Photo: Werner Forman.

170 Painted ivory head, from Nimrud. Baghdad Museum. Photo: Courtesy British School of Archaeology in Iraq.

171 Bronze bowl, from Nimrud. British Museum. Photo: Courtesy Trustees of the British Museum.

172 Bronze bowl, from Nimrud. British Museum. Photo: Courtesy Trustees of the British Museum.

173 Painted ivory plaque, from Nimrud. British Museum. Photo: Eileen Tweedy.

174 Side of an ivory box, from the 'Ziwiye Treasure'. Teheran Museum. Photo: Josephine Powell.

175 Side of an ivory box, from Nimrud. British Museum. Photo: Courtesy Trustees of the British Museum.

176 Ivory openwork plaque, from Nimrud. British Museum. Photo: Eileen Tweedy.

177 Colossal statue of a king, from Malatya. Ankara Museum. Photo: Josephine Powell.

178 Relief from a gateway at Malatya. Ankara Museum. Photo: Josephine Powell.

179 Statue of a god-king on a throne, from Carchemish. Statue now lost. Base in Ankara Museum; one lion's head in the British Museum. Photo: Courtesy Trustees of the British Museum.

180 'Caryatid' figure from Tell Halaf. Staatliche Museen, Berlin. Photo: Courtesy Bildarchiv-Foto-Marburg.

181 Rock relief, Ivriz. Photo: Seton Lloyd.

182 Sphinx at Alaca Hüyük. Photo: Josephine Powell.

183 Relief from Carchemish. Ankara Museum. Photo: Josephine Powell.

184 Relief from Karatepe (Aslantash). Photo: Dursun Cankut, courtesy of Dr Halet Cambal.

185 Relief from Karatepe (Aslantash). Photo: Dursun Cankut, courtesy of Dr Halet Cambal.

186 Bronze *situla* in the shape of a lion's head from Gordium. Ankara Museum. Painting by Piet de Jong. Photo: Courtesy Professor Rodney S. Young.

187 Pottery from the 'Child's Tumulus', Gordium. Ankara Museum. Photo: Josephine Powell.

188 Phrygian terracotta relief, from Pazarli. Ankara Museum. Photo: Josephine Powell.

189 Relief from Carchemish. Ankara Museum. Photo: Josephine Powell.

190 Bull from the 'Ishtar Gate', Babylon. Staatliche Museen, Berlin. Photo: Staatliche Museen.

191 Reconstruction of the 'Ishtar Gate', Babylon. Staatliche Museen, Berlin. Photo: Staatliche Museen.

192 Neo-Babylonian cylinder-seal. British Museum. Photo: Courtesy Trustees of the British Museum.

193 Heads of two pins, from Luristan. Teheran Museum. Photo: Josephine Powell.

194 Rein-ring, from Luristan. Louvre. Photo: Archives Photographiques.

195 Talisman, from Luristan. Teheran Museum. Photo: Josephine Powell.

196 Talisman, from Luristan. Teheran Museum. Photo: Josephine Powell.

197 Cheek-pieces, from Luristan. Boston Museum of Fine Arts. Photo: Boston Museum.

198 Bronze votive effigy from Payravand. Paris Market, 1931, present location unknown. Photo: after A. Upham Pope, *A Survey of Persian Art*, 1938, pl. 73 D.

199 Axe-head, from Luristan. Teheran Museum. Photo: Josephine Powell.

200 Bronze cheek-pieces with bit from Luristan. Teheran Museum. Photo: Josephine Powell.

201 Detail of a gold cup, from Hasanlu. Teheran Museum. Photo: Josephine Powell.

202 Relief from the treasury at Persepolis. Photo: Oriental Institute, University uf Chicago.

203 Reliefs from the stairway to the 'Tripylon' at Persepolis. Photo: Oriental Institute, University of Chicago.

204 Relief, from Persepolis. Boston Museum of Fine Arts. Photo: Boston Museum.

205 Glazed-brick-relief of a griffin, from Susa. Louvre. Photo: M. Chuzeville.

206 Glazed-brick-relief of warriors, from Susa. Louvre. Photo: M. Chuzeville.

207 Double-bull capital, from Persepolis. Oriental Institute, University of Chicago. Photo: Oriental Institute.

208 Double-bull capital from Susa. Louvre. Photo: M. Chuzeville.

209 Face of a bull-man on a capital, from Persepolis. Oriental Institute, University of Chicago. Photo: Oriental Institute.

210 Rhyton, finials, and bowl, from an unlocated Achaemenian treasure. Teheran Museum. Photo: Josephine Powell.

211 Griffin rhyton, from the 'Oxus Treasure'. British Museum. Photo: John R. Freeman.

212 Achaemenian silver figure of a man Provenance unknown. British Museum. Photo: Courtesy Trustees of the British Museum.

213 Gold bracelet, from the 'Oxus Treasure'. Victoria and Albert Museum, London. Photo: Crown Copyright reserved.

214 Achaemenian cylinder-seals. British Museum. Photo: Courtesy Trustees of the British Museum.

215 Achaemenian gold dagger. Teheran Museum. Photo: Josephine Powell. *The drawings in the Outline of Architecture have been prepared by A. E. Oral, P. P. Pratt, and M. E. Weaver.*

216 Hassuna, level IV; reconstruction of a farm-house. After Seton Lloyd.

217 Tepe Gawra, level XIII; temple, Al 'Ubaid period. After Herget.

218 Eridu; Uruk period temple. After Seton Lloyd.

219 Warka; mosaics in the Pillared Hall. After Heinrich.

220 Sakkara, reconstruction of the entrance colonnade. After Edwards.

221 Tell 'Uqair; reconstruction of altar and frescoes. After Seton Lloyd.

222 Sakkara; entrance colonnade. Photo: Max Hirmer.

223 Sakkara; reconstruction of Zoser's pyramid complex. After Lauer.

224 Sakkara; capital from Zoser's tomb area. Photo: George W. Allen.

225 Sakkara; fluted columns of Zoser's temple. Photo: George W. Allen.

226 Giza; pyramids. Photo: Max Hirmer.

227 Giza; reconstruction of the 'Great Pyramid'. After Sorrell.

291

228 Khafaje; reconstruction of the temple oval. After Darby.

229 Ur; reconstruction of Ur Nammu's *ziggurat*. After Woolley.

230 'Aqarquf; *ziggurat* as surviving. Photo: Directorate General of Antiquities, Iraq.

231 Ischali; reconstruction of the temple of Ishtar Kititum. After Hill.

232 Karnak; 'Great Hall', temple of Amon. Photo: George W. Allen.

233 Karnak; south half of the temple of Amon. Photo: George W. Allen.

234 Assur; reconstruction of the city. After Andrae.

235 Karnak; temple of Amon. Photo: Max Hirmer.

236 Karnak; plan of the temple of Amon. After Chevrier.

237 Deir-el-Bahri; Queen Hatshepsut's temple. Photo: George W. Allen.

238 Deir-el-Bahri; reconstruction of Queen Hatshepsut's temple. After Steindorff and Wolf.

239 Thebes; funerary temple of Ramesses II. Photo: Max Hirmer.

240 Tell-el-Amarnah; reconstruction of a house. After Seton Lloyd.

241 Boghazköy; plan of Temple I. After Naumann.

242 Boghazköy; reconstruction of city-walls. After Naumann.

243 Khorsabad; reconstruction of part of the citadel. After Altman.

244 Sinjerli; reconstruction. After Naumann.

245 Tell Tayanat; plan of the palace. After the plan in the Oriental Institute, University of Chicago.

246 Naqsh-i-Rustam; Achaemenian royal tomb. Photo: Oriental Institute, University of Chicago.

247 Persepolis; audience-hall of Darius and Xerxes. Photo: Oriental Institute, University of Chicago.

248 Persepolis; 'Hall of the Hundred Columns', reconstruction of portico.

249 Persepolis; relief from the 'Hall of the Hundred Columns'. Photo: Oriental Institute, University of Chicago.

Index

297

Mesopotamia, 25–6, 36, 38, 41, 66, 78, 81, 109, 115; Al 'Ubaid phase, 25; art of, 36, 38, 43, 118; brick-buildings, 268–9; craftsmanship of, 85; cultural development of, 19; highlands overrun, 233; history of, 193; motif, *197*; Protoliterate period, 18, 25; sculptors of, 101; seal-carving of, 98; writing, art of, 26

Metal-workers, metallic finish to reliefs, 246, *209*; Urartian, 224–5

Midas, tomb of, at Gordium with siren heads, 225

Middle Bronze Age, 137

Middle Kingdom art, 115–16, 118, 121, 124, 128, 129, 157, 162, 167

Minet-el-Beida, ivory lid of a box, *116*

Minoan costume, 165

Monumental lions, 130

Mosaics, coloured terracotta cones, 259, *219*; lapis-lazuli, 85; pencil-like cones, 45

Mosul, embroidery, 204

Moulded bricks, 133

Mud, used for building, 257

Mycenaean fresco, *136*

Mykerinus, limestone head of, *33*; pair-statue with his Queen, *27*

Mythological subjects, *201*

Nabonidus, defeat by Cyrus, 232

Nabopolassar, 229

Nakht, feast from the tomb of, *141*

Naqada, *7*, *10*

Naqsh-i-Rustam, Achaemenian royal tomb, *246*

Naramsin, famous stela of, 232, *71*; victory of, 106

Narmer, King, 34; alabaster ape of, 38; palette, 32, 34, 35, 64, *14*

Near East, 17, 48, 56, 111; Near Eastern man, artistic expression, 20

Neb-Amon, last rites before tomb of, *135*; painting from tomb of, *122*; scenes of feasting, *123*

Nebuchadnezzar, 229; cylinder-seals,

298

232, *192*; terracottas, 232; throne-room, 230; 'Writing on the Wall, The', 232

Necklaces, 250

Negro girl, carrying a jar, *124*

Nekhen, see Hierakonopolis

Neolithic period, 17; farmers, 17; use of sun-dried bricks, 207

New Kingdom, art, 151, 168–9; tombs, 155

Nihavand, painted jar, *4*

Nile, seasonal flooding, 56; artists of, 63; granite and limestone quarries, 101; Valley, 256

Nimrud (Caleh), Assyrians crossing river on inflated skins, *158*; capital moved to, 194; earliest group of reliefs, 194; ivories, Ethiopian slain by lion, *173*; ivory panel with Egyptian influence, *175*; reliefs with stereo-scopic effect, *158*

Nineveh, 84, 106; abandoned by Sargon, 194; defeat of the Elamites, *165*; fall of, 229; group of reliefs, 194, *146–9*, *160*; Küyünjik palace-mound, 204; rebuilt by Sennacherib and Assur-banipal, *160*, *164–9*

Ningal, statue of, 88

Ningirsu, granite figure, 88

Nippur, 129

Nofretiti, head of, *147*; portrait-bust of, *144*

'Nomads' gear', 235

North Syria, 137

Nuzi, Mitannian city, 133; boar's head from, *106*; Mitannian painted pottery, *107*

Obelisk, *235*

Old Kingdom, art, 62, 78; mortuary sculpture, 68

Old Testament prophets, 229

Ornaments, papyrus and lotus, *233*

Orontes Valley, 214

'Orthostats', Carchemish, *183*; sculp-tured, 220–1

Ur, famous head-dresses, 104; First Dynasty tombs, 84; gold bull's head, 89; gold dagger, *56*; gold wig-helmet of Mes-kalam-shar, *53*; gold vase, *55*; head-dress of a woman, *54*; 'Inlaid Standard', *46-7*, 87, 89; ornamental rein-ring of a wild ass, 92, *58*; 'Ram caught in the thicket, The', 95, *57*; 'Royal Cemetery', 84, 104; Third Dynasty, 129; Ur III, 129

Ur Nammu's *ziggurat* at Ur, *229*
Urartu, 224; Urartian, 224-5
Urnanshe, ruler of Lagash, 87; stela of, *49*
Uruk, *see* Warka
User-het, hunting scene from tomb of, *134*; painting from tomb of, *150*

Vaulted tombs, 129
Vessels, drinking-horn, 250; gold, 250; painted *187*
Votive effigy, *198*

Walls, adorning of palace, 194; crenellated, 230; defensive of Boghazköy, 273, *242*; painting on, Sargon II, throne-room, *159*; Sumerian ornamented, 265, 268
Warka (ancient Uruk), 36, 43, 45, 129; alabaster vase, *18*; cone mosaic, *24*; façade ornament, *104*; female face in white marble, *21-2*; granite, 36, *17*; pillared hall, *219-20*

'Warrior Gate', 141
Water-carriers, *133*
Weaving, shown on sculpture, 204
Wooden harps, Ur 'Standard', 89
Woolley, Sir Leonard, 89, 147
'Workshop figures', 183
'Writing on the Wall, The', 232

Xerxes, heir-apparent of Darius, *202*

Yarimlim, King of Orontes, 147; head of, *115*
Yazilikaya, Hittite carvings at, *113-14*
Young girl, ivory, *132*

Zagros, Iranian art in valleys of, 233
Zebu, Indian humped bull, 88, *51*
Ziggurat, 83, 229; Aqarquf, *230*; basic plan, 265, *231*; Birs Nimrod, 'The Tower of Babel', 265; Choga Zambil, 233; Etemenanki's and Marduk's, ('Tower of Babel'), 230; 'staged towers', 129, 132; Ur Nammu's, at Ur, *229*
'Ziwiye, Treasure of', 174
Zoser, capital of tomb, *224*; first King of the Third Dynasty, 66, 68; tomb at Sakkara, 70; fluted pilasters, 264; funerary buildings, 260-4, *223-5*; 'Hall of Pillars', *222*; limestone jointed tomb, 264; statue of, *38*; structural ornament of tomb, 226

The World of Art Library

History of Art

Artists

Galleries

THE NATIONAL GALLERY LONDON *Sir Philip Hendy*
THE TATE GALLERY *Sir John Rothenstein*
THE LOUVRE *Germain Bazin*
IMPRESSIONIST PAINTINGS IN THE LOUVRE *Germain Bazin*
THE SCHOOL OF PARIS (MUSÉE D'ART MODERNE) *Bernard Dorival*
THE PRADO *Sanchez Canton*
DUTCH MUSEUMS *R. Van Luttervelt*
THE DRESDEN GALLERY *Henner Menz*
THE HERMITAGE *Pierre Descargues*
THE NATIONAL GALLERY WASHINGTON *John Walker*
THE UFFIZI AND PITTI *Filippo Rossi*

General

A CONCISE HISTORY OF ART (2 vols.) *Germain Bazin*
THE ARTS OF MAN *Eric Newton*
ENCYCLOPAEDIA OF OLD MASTERS *Joachim Fernau*
A CONCISE HISTORY OF PAINTING:
FROM GIOTTO TO CÉZANNE *Michael Levey*
THE WORLD OF THE IMPRESSIONISTS *François Mathey*
PRIMITIVE ART *Douglas Fraser*
MASTERS OF THE JAPANESE PRINT *Richard Lane*
GRAPHIC ART OF THE 18TH CENTURY *Jean Adhémar*
GRAPHIC ART OF THE 19TH CENTURY *Claude Roger-Marx*
ENCYCLOPAEDIA OF MODERN ARCHITECTURE edited by *Wolfgang Pehnt*
A CONCISE HISTORY OF BALLET *F. Reyna*
A CONCISE HISTORY OF PHOTOGRAPHY *Helmut and Alison Gernsheim*

Details of paperback editions of this series can be obtained from your bookseller

THAMES AND HUDSON 30 Bloomsbury Street, London, W.C.1